VOL. 52

THE ST MICHAEL'S HILL PRECINCT OF THE UNIVERSITY OF BRISTOL

THE TOPOGRAPHY OF MEDIEVAL AND EARLY MODERN BRISTOL, PART 2

DEDICATION

THIS special Bristol Record Society volume is respectfully dedicated to Dr. Joseph Bettey FRHist, FSA and Mr. David Large with grateful thanks for their long and distinguished service to the Society.

Joseph Bettey succeeded Professor Patrick McGrath in 1989 as General Editor of the Bristol Record Society and has since been instrumental in consolidating its international reputation for publications of a high standard of scholarship. Dr. Bettey, who retired as Reader in Local History from the University of Bristol in 1994, has written widely on early modern British history and has made a particularly significant contribution to our understanding of Bristol's history. He edited Vol. 25 on the *Correspondence of the Smyth Family 1548-1642* in 1982 and delivered a public lecture for the Society the following year which was published as *Church and Community in the Sixteenth Century*. With the assistance of his wife Valerie, he has laboured tirelessly on the Society's behalf, patiently coaxing work from a wide array of scholars and ensuring the Society was always on a sound financial footing. His legacy is an enduring one, but his example will be hard to emulate.

David Large has served with great distinction as the Society's Secretary for many years, presiding with energy and decision over its Annual General Meetings. He has also edited two well-received Bristol Record Society volumes, *The Port of Bristol 1848-1884* (BRS Vol. 36) and *The Municipal Government of Bristol 1851-1901* (BRS Vol. 50). In 1981 he gave the Society's first public lecture which was published by the Society as *Radicalism in Bristol in the Nineteenth Century*. Mr. Large retired as Senior Lecturer in History in 1986 from the University of Bristol. During a career spanning nearly thirty years he wrote on many aspects of Bristol's past including Irish immigration and public health policy.

'The North East View of Prince Rupert's Fort, commonly called the ROYAL FORT',
James Stewart, April 10th 1752

THE ST MICHAEL'S HILL PRECINCT OF THE UNIVERSITY OF BRISTOL :

MEDIEVAL AND EARLY MODERN TOPOGRAPHY

BY

ROGER H LEECH

Published by
BRISTOL RECORD SOCIETY
in association with
THE UNIVERSITY OF BRISTOL
2000

ISBN 0 901538 22 1

The Bristol Record Society is indebted to the University of Bristol for its support for this volume and acknowledges with thanks the continued support of Bristol City Council, the University of Bristol, the Bristol and West Building Society and the Society of Merchant Venturers. It is also pleased to welcome the support of the University of the West of England.

BRISTOL RECORD SOCIETY

The Society exists to encourage the preservation, study and publication of documents relating to the history of Bristol, and since its foundation in 1929 has published fifty-one major volumes of historic documents concerning the city. All the volumes, together with their authoritative introductions, are edited by scholars who are experts in the chosen field.

Recent volumes have included: *William Worcestre: the Topography of Modern Bristol*; *The Goldney Family: a Bristol Merchant Dynasty*; and *Bristol, Africa and the Eighteenth Century Slave Trade to America, 1770-1807*.

Forthcoming volumes will include All Saints' Records Part 2; the papers of Edward Southwell; Atlantic Trade Documents.

In return for the modest subscription, members of the Society receive the volumes as they are published. The subscription for private members is £10 per annum, for UK institutions £12.50, and for Overseas membership £15.

Subscriptions and enquiries should be made to the Hon. Secretaries, c/o The School of History, University of the West of England, St Matthias Campus, Oldbury Court Road, Bristol BS16 2JP.

Produced for the Society by
J. W. Arrowsmith Ltd.
Winterstoke Road,
Bristol BS3 2NT

CONTENTS

LIST OF ILLUSTRATIONS

20. Gate formerly adjacent to Ivy Cottage (author)
21. John Elbridge's school, James Stewart, 1747 (Bodleian Library, Western MSS, Gough Somerset 2, fol.13)
22. John Elbridge's school, plan of 1767 (BRO DC E/40/25 52157)
23. Oldbury House, St Michael's Hill, in 1999 (author)
24. Eusebius Brookes's house, from St Michael's Hill (Oldbury House on left) (BRSMG N.109)
25. Eusebius Brookes's house, from the rear (Oldbury House on right) (BRSMG M.1734)
26. Bartholomew lands, as shown on plan of 1791; St Michael's Hill runs from south-east to north-west, see Fig.13 for location (BRO 00568(9))
27. The Royal Fort, Millerd, 1673
28. The Royal Fort, Rocque, 1742
29. The 'Manor House' (University Library, Special Collections)
30. The 'Manor House' from the rear (University Library, Special Collections)
31. Low and high parts of Cromwell House in 1752, Manor House on left (Bodleian Library, Western MSS, Gough Somerset 2, fol.15)
32. Richard Garway's house, 1752 (Bodleian Library, Western MSS, Gough Somerset 2, fol.14)
33. House to south of gate, 1752 (Bodleian Library, Western MSS, Gough Somerset 2, fol.15)
34. Nos. 53–57 St Michael's Hill (University Library, Special Collections)
35 No. 59 St Michael's Hill (University Library, Special Collections)
36. Plan of Tinkers' Close, c.1735–55 (BRO AC/JS (8))
37. Park Gate House, 1950s (BRO 20894)
38. Tankard's Close, looking north to the Distillhouse (on left) (University Library, Special Collections)
39. Nos. 23-9 St Michael's Hill, 1999 (author)
40. Nos. 31–7 St Michael's Hill, c.1813 (BRO 04479(3) fol.63a)
41. Nos. 39–41 St Michael's Hill, 1861 (BRO 38041/BMC/12/PL12 fol.60)
42. Nos. 39–57 St Michael's Hill from the rear, 1950s (University Library, Special Collections)
43. Llan House and Rupert house, drawing of the early twentieth century (BCL)
44. Nos. 1–3 Lower Church Lane, 1887 (BRO 17346)
45. Nos. 1–3 Lower Park Hill, 1779 (University Deeds 251)
46. Corner of Lower Park Hill and Medical Avenue, 1818 (University Deeds 251)
47. Nos. 3–4 Old Park from the rear, 1920s (BRSMG, glass plate negatives)
48. Old Park Hill, street frontage (University Library, Special Collections)
49. Old Park Hill, detached kitchen to rear (University Library, Special Collections)

50. Park Lane / St Michael's churchyard, Gilbert Moore's house, drawing of late nineteenth century (BRSMG M.4023)
51. The Manor House, Park Lane, 1950s (BRO 20894)
52. Richard Jordan's house, Millerd, 1673
53. Pear Tree Cottage, Park Lane, 1950s (BRO 20894)
54. Nos. 3-4 Stile Lane, (BCL Loxton drawings X.1761)
55. No. 4 Stile Lane, 1932 (Winstone 1979 (107))
56. No. 4 Stile Lane, plan of 1808 (University Deeds 252)
57. Nos. 1–4 Upper Church Lane, 1784 (BRO A22026/1)
58. Park Row, 1864: from left to right above Park Row are nos. 8 and 9 (semi-detached pair), no. 12 (gabled), and nos. 13 and 14 (both eighteenth century), then no. 15 Lunsford House, and finally part of no. 16 (Winstone 1972 (9); Reece Winstone Archive)
59. No. 10 Park Row, gabled house on left, 1957 (Winstone 1988, 254; Reece Winstone Archive)
60. Tower View in 1796 (University Deeds 243)
61. Tower View in 2000 (author)
62. Lunsford House in 2000 (author)
63. Nos. 16 and 17 Park Row, detail from watercolour of the Red Lodge and Lodge Street, 1824 (BRSMG M.2571)
64. No. 17 Park Row, one of the two houses in front of the main house (BRSMG M.2561)

Note: illustrations 9, 10, 12 and 13 may be freely copied and enlarged for educational or private study

ACKNOWLEDGEMENTS

Thanks are due first to David Adamson, the former bursar of the University of Bristol, now Estates Officer to the University of Cambridge, for his initiative and encouragement in commissioning this study. His erstwhile colleagues have much assisted the progress of the work, and I must especially thank Mike Phipps the present Bursar, Jenny Crew, whose help in providing access to the deeds has been immense, and Tony Roberts for his unrivalled knowledge of the University's building archives. In the University Library Michael Richardson and Hannah Lowery have provided a range of information which has proved invaluable to the study. Outside the precincts of the University its title deeds are to be found in part in the holding of Veale Wasbrough, solicitors; here I must thank Wayne Thomas for facilitating the examination of this collection.

Linked to this study has been the commencement of an archaeological survey of the Royal Fort and its surroundings. Here I must thank Mark Horton of the Department of Archaeology in the University of Bristol for his most generous assistance and valued advice, at the same time thanking Jon Bull and James Andrews of the University of Southampton Department of Earth Sciences for organising the geophysical survey work. The author must also thank Joe Bettey for much helpful comment; the idea of a Bristol Record Society series of volumes on the topography of the city was his inspiration and here his work on the Royal Fort has proved invaluable; it should be consulted by anyone looking into the history of the Royal Fort and Tyndall's Park (Bettey 1997). I must also thank Martin Crossley Evans, both of the University and the Bristol Record Society, for many helpful comments on the draft text.

The documentary research for this study would not have been possible without the assistance of a number of institutions, first and foremost of these being the Bristol Record Office. John Williams and his staff are warmly thanked for all their help in this area. Also much appreciated has been the assistance of staff of the Bristol City Museum and Art Gallery and the Bristol Reference Library for access to material in their collections. In the British Library the examination of the Harleian Charters was much assisted by the work of Bridget Jones of the former Royal Commission on the Historical Monuments of England, now part of English Heritage.

The work of the former Royal Commission was directed towards the compilation of a forthcoming study of the town houses of the City of Bristol (Leech forthcoming). My understanding of the historic buildings within the University Precinct has also been immeasurably enhanced through the comments and advice of colleagues formerly in the Commission and now in English Heritage, most especially John Cattell, Nigel Fradgley and Barry Jones. Interpretations of particular buildings are derived from this work in preparation.

Underlying all this work has been the ongoing support of the City Archaeologist Bob Jones and his assistant Jon Brett. This and the access provided to the Urban Archaeological Database have been much appreciated. I must also express my appreciation to the general editors, Madge Dresser and Peter Fleming, for their advice, and to Victoria Arrowsmith-Brown for much patience and assistance in seeing the volume through the press. Finally I must thank Pamela Leech for all her much valued assistance in the preparation of this study.

The Bristol Record Society and the University of Bristol are grateful to the following for permission to reproduce illustrations: Bodleian Library, University of Oxford, frontispiece, 18, 19, 21, 31, 32, 33; Bristol City Museum and Art Gallery, dustjacket, 24, 25, 47, 50, 63, 64; Trustees of Bristol Municipal Charities, 41; Bristol Record Office, 26, 36, 37, 40, 41, 44, 51, 53, 57; Diocese of Bristol, 15, 16, 22; Reece Winstone Archive, 58, 59.

EDITORIAL NOTES

1. All alphanumeric references not prefixed with a source or location are to material in the Bristol Record Office.
2. Bibliographic references cited in the text refer to the Bibliography following the tenement histories.
3. Christian names have generally been standardised throughout, surnames are usually as cited in the original texts.
4. Unless otherwise noted, individuals cited from deeds and analogous documents are described as of Bristol.
5. The post-medieval term 'Corporation' has generally been substituted for other often earlier terms occurring in the sources, such as 'mayor and commonalty' and 'chamber'.
6. All references to 1775 are to Sketchley's Directory unless otherwise indicated.
7. References for Section 1 are cited only when the information is not readily available from the relevant parts of Section 2.
8. In Section 2 the sources for the entries *Occupancy from the ratebooks* are tax and rate assessments for 1662 onwards, all in the Bristol Record Office.

ABBREVIATIONS USED IN THE TEXT

ft and ins	feet and inches
BCL	Bristol City Library
BL	British Library
BRO	Bristol Record Office
BRS	Bristol Record Society volumes
BRSMG	Bristol City Museum and Art Gallery
GRB	Great Red Book (Parts 1–4), BRS vols 4, 8, 13 and 16
GRO	Gloucestershire Record Office
GWB	Great White Book, BRS vol 32
Latimer Annals	Annals of Bristol, John Latimer, Kingsmead Reprints, 3 volumes, 1970
L & P	Letters and Papers, Foreign and Domestic, Henry VIII (21 vols. and addenda, London, 1864–1932)
LRB	Little Red Book, ed. Bickley 1900
PRO	Public Record Office
RCHME	The former Royal Commission on the Historical Monuments of England
SRO	Somerset Record Office
SRS	Somerset Record Society volumes
Suff RO	Suffolk Record Office
TBGAS	Transactions of the Bristol and Gloucestershire Archaeological Society
UBHT	United Bristol Healthcare Trust

FOREWORD

In broad terms this report follows the format adopted for the Bristol Record Society volume 48, *The topography of medieval and early modern Bristol, part 1: property holdings in the early walled town and Marsh suburb north of the Avon.* This study in effect provides the text for the part of the parish of St Michael that lies between Park Row and St Michael's Hill (Fig.1). The rationale behind such a study as set out in the above need not be restated here, except to say firstly that this study has extended the scope of such work by including much more information on the occupancy of properties through time, utilising assessments and rates of the seventeenth and eighteenth centuries extensively. In this study Tinkers' or Tankard's Close is the only area not covered by such work.

The purpose of this study as defined for the University of Bristol was to provide an understanding of the historical archaeology contained within the St Michael's Hill precinct, excluding the small area of Tyndall's Park Road which lay within the ancient parish of Westbury upon Trym. It was thought from the outset that research would reveal a context extending from the merely local to considerations of global importance, the role of Bristol's citizens in what Charles Orser has termed the four 'haunts' of historical archaeology: colonialism, Eurocentrism, capitalism and modernity, and through them the shaping of the modern world (Orser 1996). The detailed research commissioned by the University has revealed the many close links between the Atlantic trade and the inhabitants of the past landscape of the St Michael's Hill precinct, most especially in the sixteenth to the eighteenth centuries.

The role of the English Civil War in the shaping of early modern England has much occupied historians. The presence of one of the largest citadels or fortresses of the English Civil War within the University Precinct has received rather less attention. This study has now provided a much firmer basis for the further investigation of this fortress, identifying its limits as rather greater than previously considered, identifying a surviving upstanding bastion and other parts of the defences, and locating various buildings that stood within the fortress. Of the last the fort well and Stuart House are intimately connected.

This study is for the most part of the period to c.1775, the terminal date adopted for the Record Society's series, on account of the existence of Sketchley's street directory of that year. In formulating the study of the archaeology of the University Precinct, it appeared likely that the early modern period, from the fifteenth to the eighteenth centuries, would be the focus of archaeological attention, the period in which the area now occupied by the precinct was centre-stage to the Atlantic trade. The archaeology of the societies touched by this trade is much studied in North America, increasingly so in Africa, but hardly at all in Europe, England and Bristol in particular. It is hoped that this study will provide a starting point for such research within the precinct of the University of Bristol. Detailed recommendations for future archaeological research have been set out in a separate report prepared for the University of Bristol by the author.

INTRODUCTION

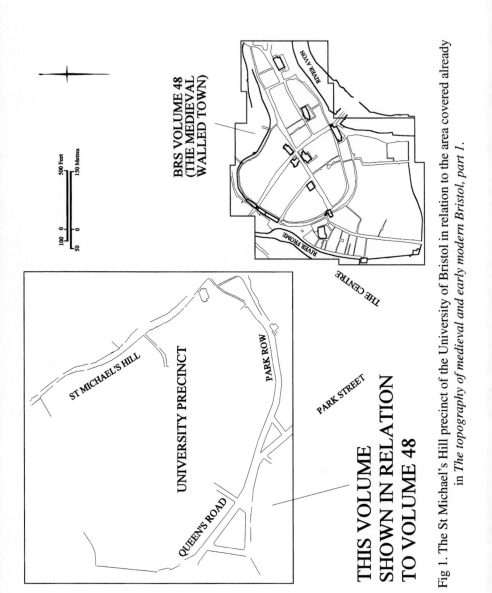

Fig 1. The St Michael's Hill precinct of the University of Bristol in relation to the area covered already in *The topography of medieval and early modern Bristol, part 1*.

THE SETTING:
AN OVERVIEW FROM THE HISTORIC MAPS

The main precinct of the University of Bristol is situated on and around the summit of St Michael's Hill to the north-west of the centre of medieval Bristol. The town of Bristol, founded c.1000 A.D., was first confined within a fortified enclosure between the Avon and the Frome, centred on the crossroads of Broad Street, Corn Street, High Street and Wine Street. The expansion of this town was rapid. Less than 150 years after its founding it was described by King Stephen's chronicler as 'almost the richest city'. By the mid thirteenth century the walled area had been greatly extended. The suburbs on the west were now closer to St Michael's Hill, and the church of St Michael's was certainly by then in existence.

The suburban expansion that took in St Michael's Hill and eventually all of what is now the University Precinct had begun by the sixteenth century. This early expansion and the landscape disturbed by the building of the Royal Fort in the English Civil War are not recorded on any surviving maps. The continued suburban expansion is most easily followed through the maps of 1673 and later. Millerd's map of 1673 (Fig.2) shows a scatter of gardens and houses, the Little Park, houses on St Michael's Hill and the houses contained within the Royal Fort, 'now demolished' and 'converted into houses and pleasant gardens'. The legend amplifies this theme: 'the riseing of the hill St Michael being converted into comely buildings & pleasant gardens makes a very beautifull addition to the suburbs thereof'.

The revised edition of Millerd's map of c.1710 (Fig.3) shows a number of new buildings and the subdivision of larger enclosures as alterations to the earlier edition of 1673. At least two new buildings and various garden features had appeared within the Little Park. On St Michael's Hill new houses had appeared on the west side. On the west three new closes had been created to the north of Park Row. South of the Royal Fort gatehouse was a new enclosed garden.

Rocque's map of 1742 (Fig.4) was the first to show almost the entire area occupied by the University Precinct. This map shows field boundaries but not, with a few exceptions, the detail of individual house plots. The map

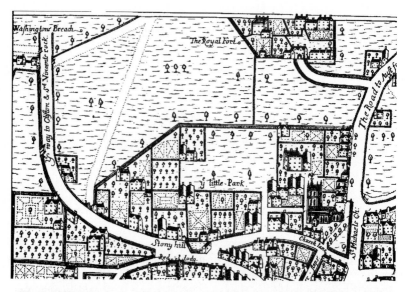

Fig 2. Millerd's map of Bristol in 1673, extract extending to the limit of the mapped area (for this and other early printed maps see *Bibliography*)

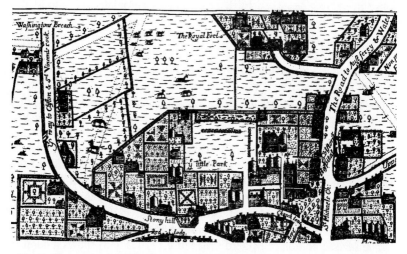

Fig 3. The revised Millerd's map of Bristol, c.1710, extract extending to the limit of the mapped area

can be extended further to the north west by adding a small section of de Wilstar's map of Clifton of 1746. Further building had taken place by this date in a number of locations, notably within the Little Park and on the west side of St Michael's Hill. To the north of the Little Park is shown the Royal Fort.

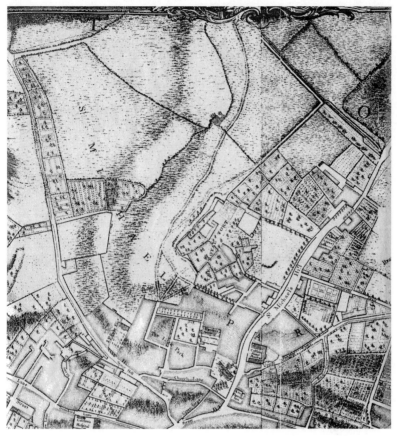

Fig 4. Rocque's map of 1742, extract extending to the limit of the
mapped area

From the mid eighteenth century other illustrative sources supplement
the historic maps. Stewart's drawings and Repton's Red Book are both
important sources of information for the changing landscape of the Royal
Fort in the 1750s and early 1800s (both sources are in the Bodleian
Library).

Donne's maps of 1773 and 1826 are less useful in showing the changing
landscape of the hillside and plateau. On the former, much of the area of
interest is concealed by the cartouche, while the details of buildings close
to the limits of the city boundary are possibly copied from Rocque's map.
Donne's map of 1826 (Fig.5) has more detail and is particularly useful for
the study of features within Tyndall's Park, for instance the ha-has. The
map of Ashmead and Plumley of 1828 is though very much more detailed
and accurate.

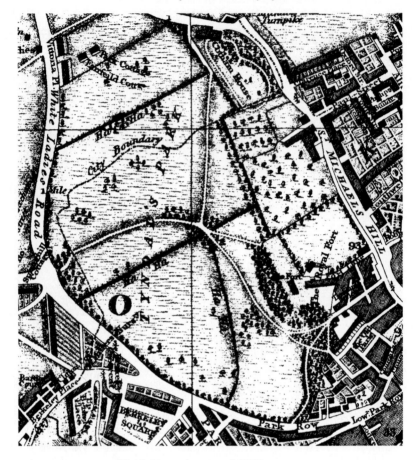

Fig 5. Donne's map of 1826, extract

The 1828 map (overleaf, Fig.6) shows the area occupied by housing much the same as in 1742. Amongst the small changes that had occurred two of the most obvious are the construction of Park Place to the west of St Michael's Hill, and the building of a row of houses in place of the single large house which had half blocked St Michael's Hill nearly opposite its junction with Paul Street. In 1828 the area of open land also remained much the same. The most obvious change was the opening up of the closes to the west of the Royal Fort to form parkland.

The first Ordnance Survey 1:2500 plan of 1885 (Fig.7, reduced from the larger more detailed plans at 1:500 published in 1884) shows a similar landscape of housing and parkland, the latter now much encroached upon since 1828. To the south-west of the reduced parkland could be seen the University College, the beginnings of the present road system encircling the Grammar School site, and the new residential roads leading into

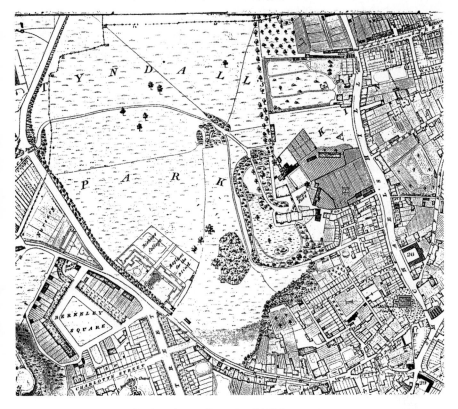

Fig 6. Ashmead's map of 1828, extract

Tyndall's Park Road. The large villas on the east side of Woodland Road must have provided an immediate contrast with the new streets of terraced housing, St Michael's Park and the streets to the north.

The second Ordnance Survey 1:2500 plan of 1903 (Fig.8) shows further developments. By this date Woodland Road had been completed, linking Park Row to the new residential streets to the north of the Grammar School. These twentieth-century developments and the subsequent expansion of the University of Bristol lie beyond the scope of this study (for the history of the University see most recently Carleton 1984; for twentieth-century and earlier buildings see Mowl 1992).

Successive maps allow us to chart the history of this landscape in general terms but not in any detail. The map of 1828 is the earliest to show most house plots. The ensuing sections use the evidence of these early maps where appropriate, but make extensive use of other documentary sources and the study of the material record, particularly that of surviving structures and that provided through archaeological research.

Fig 7. Ordnance Survey map of
1885, extract

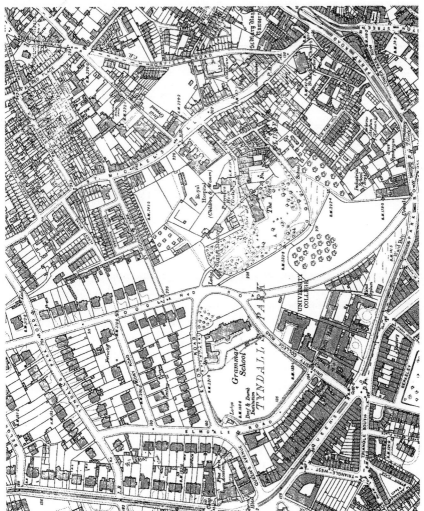

Fig 8. Ordnance Survey map of 1903, extract

THE MEDIEVAL AND EARLY POST-MEDIEVAL LANDSCAPE

In the medieval period the University Precinct was an area largely of fields and closes, bounded by roads which remain in use to this day on the south and east (Fig.9). The outline of this landscape can be reconstructed from documents and early maps, utilising techniques of town plan analysis.

The south side of the precinct is now defined in part by Park Row. In the sixteenth and seventeenth centuries, Lower Park Row, Park Row and the road around the lower side of The Triangle were known as the road from Bristol to Clifton. The continuation of this road to Clifton was the upper part of Jacob's Well Road, known in the charter of 1373 by those defining the city boundaries as 'Wodewilleslane'. The east side of the precinct is defined by St Michael's Hill, another ancient route, also mentioned in the 1373 charter, known then as 'the road from Bristol to Hembury' (BRS 1, 154–7).

Extending up the slopes above Park Row and across the plateau towards what is now Tyndall's Park Road was a landscape of small fields and closes. A short distance to the south of what is now Tyndall's Park Road, the boundaries of several of these fields were noted by those defining the city boundaries in 1373. From the corner of 'Bartholomeu is clos' the boundary passed 'along the ditch of the same field northwards on the western part of the same ditch as far as a stone fixed in the corner of a certain close called Fockynggrove; and from thence directly eastwards along a certain long ditch from stone to stone as far as a stone fixed in the northern corner of a certain close called Cantockes clos; and from thence along the ditch of the same close directly eastwards on the northern part of the same ditch as far as a stone fixed at the eastern corner of a certain croft of the houses of the religious of Magdalen and Bartholomew of Bristol; and from thence directly southwards along the ditch of the same croft as far as another stone fixed in another corner of the same croft; and from thence directly along another hedge eastwards on the northern part of the same croft as far as the king's highway which leads from Bristol towards Hembury' (ibid.).

The charter defining the city boundaries provides fortuitously a glimpse of what was visible in 1373, a landscape of hedges, ditches, boundary stones, and the occasional lane or road leading out of the city. The charter also provides a number of known points which facilitate the reconstruction and analysis of a now largely vanished landscape. Boundaries and boundary stones are shown from Rocque's map of 1742 onwards.

Closest to St Michael's Hill were a number of roughly rectangular fields or closes. The relationships in plan between these indicate that some were earlier than others. Opposite the nunnery of St Mary Magdalen was the churchyard and church of St Michael, first mentioned in the 1190s; the parsonage or vicarage had been built in one corner of the churchyard by 1479, possibly at a much earlier date (references to this and other individual properties are given in Section 2).

In plan the churchyard was abutted by a block of properties fronting St Michael's Hill and extending as far north as no. 51; at least a part of this block had been developed for housing by the later fifteenth century. The four timber-framed houses nos. 23–29 immediately above the church are of the seventeenth century and are first recorded in 1637; but further uphill nos. 31–41 are built on the sites of houses recorded in the 1480s. Nos. 43–51 occupy the sites of houses existing in the 1690s.

Abutting both the churchyard and the block of properties that is now nos. 23–51 St Michael's Hill was the estate known by the later seventeenth century as the Little Park (see Section 2, Part 8 for references). This existed as a distinct entity by c.1400 when it was the property of the Cheddar family. 'Warresclos', first mentioned in a lease of 1402, was possibly the whole or a greater part of this holding.

Abutting the Little Park were further closes or gardens fronting Park Row. These certainly existed by the mid fifteenth century. By 1463–4 no. 29 Park Row consisted of a house or barn and a garden; the property to the east, of uncertain extent, existed as a separate entity by c.1491.

Further enclosures extended northwards on the west side of St Michael's Hill. To the north of the Little Park, abutting both it and nos. 23–51 St Michael's Hill, was Tinkers' Close. This was possibly the garden held by John Canynges in 1405; it was certainly known as 'Broome Hay' by 1619. To the north was Joachim's Close, two later two closes, belonging to St Augustine's Abbey. This was possibly part of the same block of properties. The western boundaries of the close were probably altered and shortened following the building of the Royal Fort; after the Civil War the land occupied by the fort appears to have been granted to the Corporation rather than reverting to its former owners. Several of the post Civil War boundaries follow the outer edge of the fort ditch, which cannot have existed as a boundary feature before 1643. To the north Magdalen Close probably existed long before the sixteenth century, being formerly of the nunnery of St Mary Magdalen. Before the Civil War Tinkers' Close,

Jochim's Lease and the properties to the north, all probably shared a common western boundary.

Beyond this western boundary at least two closes extended the enclosed area further to the west. One was Wimble Close, the site of a windmill owned by the Corporation, to the west of Jochim's Lease in 1619, and most probably on the summit of the hill later occupied by the Royal Fort. To the north, sharing the same boundary on the west, was a close formerly of St Bartholomew's Priory; its outline was not shown on Rocque's map of 1742, but its limits were still shown in 1743 and 1811 by boundary stones recorded on contemporary plans.

Collectively these enclosures on the west side of St Michael's Hill provide evidence for a succession of enclosure initiatives, of unknown date but of before the fifteenth century. The landscape that emerged was one of small rectangular enclosures, some certainly enclosed by stone walls.

Much further to the west on the north side of the road to Clifton the process of enclosure produced a very different landscape. The four fields identified as Bartholomew Close, the King's Orchard, Inner Puckingrove and Hither Puckingrove can be argued from plan-analysis to be sub-divisions of one large enclosure, irregularly defined away from the road. This subdivision of a larger enclosure must have occurred before the 1280s, when the King's Orchard was first recorded.

Cantock's Close was situated between these two areas of enclosure, possibly the relict part of a much larger open space bounded only by the road to Clifton, St Michael's Hill and the city boundary. Cantock's Close probably existed in its contracted form by the early thirteenth century, by which date most of the endowments of St Augustine's Abbey had been made (see ed. Walker 1998, xxx-xxxi). In this form the straight northern boundary of Cantock's Close, the city boundary from 1373, continued eastwards as the northern limit of Magdalen Close and the enclosures closer to St Michael's Hill. A straight boundary on a very similar alignment, always in the parish of Westbury upon Trym, continued eastwards beyond the east side of St Michael's Hill.

The documentary sources do not give a clear picture of when and how citizens first made use of these fields and closes for gardens as detached adjuncts to their city dwellings. There are indications that this was happening by the fifteenth century.

The early medieval and earlier history of this landscape cannot be learnt through the study of the documentary sources. Only archaeological research could determine if this pattern of fields and closes had its origins in the subdivision of the land in the Roman and earlier period. Palaeo-environmental research might also provide much information on early land use and ecology.

Dwellings

In the Little Park estate one house had been built by 1531, probably that described in 1596 as a 'Capitall Messuage or Mansion House' with gardens to east and west, then sold to Robert Aldworth. From 1602 this was owned by Hugh Murcot, a vintner, then by his widow. By 1660 it belonged to Isaac Harper, owner of the Little Park Estate. The mansion house (later nos. 1–2 and no. 3 Lower Park Hill) was on both sides of Lower Park Hill, the street originating as the entry through the street door and pavement into the park. To the east Upper Church Lane led directly from the mansion house to St Michael's church. Access to a property in the Little Park was in 1710 still cited as being through 'the street door' and 'pavement' of this house. The 'large ruinous messuage' mentioned in a deed of 1754 for the west end of Lower Church Lane was probably part of the mansion house of 1596.

By the 1640s at least two houses had been built to the west of the Little Park. By 1548 the property formerly of Mede's chantry and later nos. 8–13 Park Row consisted of a close, two gardens and a lodge, the last probably the second residence of a wealthy citizen, a building type that was to become far more numerous after the Civil War. This lodge stood until the 1950s.

Further west another house had been built by John Jones mariner before 1604 in Cantock's Close on the north side of Park Row. This too became the residence of a wealthy citizen. George Lane, who died here in 1613, had become a merchant in 1585 and was made a member of the Spanish Company in 1605. His principal residence in St Werburgh's parish was typical of those of the ruling and merchant élite, its principal room a hall, probably open to the roof, and bedecked with weaponry signifying Lane's status in the militia and city. His house in Cantock's Close, described in the inventory of his possessions as the 'house att the hill' was more simply furnished, both as a retreat from the city and as a working farm or smallholding. Venetian dining glasses, a lute and books were clearly for pleasure. Equipment for butter and cheese making, beehives for honey and tools for haymaking went hand in hand with the possession of eleven cows and a bull, five pigs and twenty eight sheep. By the time of the Civil War Lane's house was owned by Philip Langley, also a wealthy merchant.

Gardens

By the beginning of the Civil War in 1642 the area occupied by the University Precinct still consisted largely of fields and closes, but was increasingly being utilised for gardens. Away from St Michael's Hill immediately above the church, only a few dwellings could probably be identified, but already several gardens had been laid out in the Little Park.

Two on the uphill side of Lower Church Lane were in 1596 held by William Ellis, an alderman of the city and by Thomas Hopkins, a merchant, the latter next to the vicarage. Further east in Park Row in 1596 was a garden held by John Barker, also a merchant, adjoining to another garden late of William Sprint.

THE CIVIL WAR AND THE ROYAL FORT

In November 1642 Bristol was occupied by the Parliamentarian forces, and the defence of the city was commenced. On the northern side of the city small forts or redoubts were built on Brandon Hill, close to Park Row (the Essex Work) and on Windmill Hill, the last necessitating the demolition of the windmill within Windmill Close. It was through the defences close to Park Row that Colonel Washington successfully breached the Parliamentary defences in July 1643. Negotiations for the Parliamentarian surrender were begun in 'a garden house, right up against the Essex Work'. This was probably the house built by John Jones and in 1613 the home of George Lane. Linking these forts was the defensive line surrounding the city, formed by a bank and ditch, described by de Gomme and located by archaeological excavation on the north side of Park Row in 1994 (BaRAS 1994, Firth 1925, Roy 1975, Russell 1995, Sprigg 1648).

The defensive line extended north-eastwards from the Royal Fort to the 'platforme by Mile [St Michael's] Hill Gate', where there was a battery of two guns in July 1643. De Gomme wrote that here 'the line crookes a little northward to fetch in' close to the house of Alderman Jones which was 'upon the Highwaye's side'; in the siege of 1643 this house was 'more than Canon proofe, and most secure against the Enemies shot'. Jones's house was probably that shown on the 1742 map as furthest out from the city on the east side of St Michael's Hill, later known as Belfield House, a small part now remaining as no. 114. Slightly to the north and on the west side of St Michael's Hill, another house shown on the same map was built by Eusebius Brookes before 1667, and was possibly built on the 'platforme' of the gate. In 1667 Brookes was given permission by the City to fill in the ditch alongside the road, which was said to be currently 'deep and dangerous'. The incorporation in a later house of the former battery controlling the entry into the town at this point could explain the narrowing of the street at this point shown on the map of 1742, rectified by the demolition of the greater part of the house in c.1828. A small part survives as Oldbury House.[1]

Following the capture of the city by the Royalist army, Prince Rupert was installed as governor in August 1643. His engineer Sir Bernard de Gomme had already been responsible for the defence of Oxford; he was therefore possibly the designer of the new fort now built to replace the small fort or redoubt on Windmill Hill. This was to serve as Prince Rupert's headquarters and became known as the Great or Royal Fort. It was the most heavily defended part of the Royalist fortifications and was surrendered by Prince Rupert to Cromwell only after the capture of most of the defences surrounding the city in September 1645. In his letter to Parliament Oliver Cromwell reported that 'the Royal Fort had victuals in it for one hundred and fifty men for three hundred and twenty days'. Following its capture the fort was further improved with the facing of the ramparts and bastions in stone. It was demolished in 1655–6 (Russell 1995, 18; Sprigg 1648, 127).

The precise outline and location of the Royal Fort has been a matter of speculation. The most recent plan is by Russell, based on a correlation of Millerd's plan with the location of the surviving gatehouse and the short length of wall in the shrubbery to the south of Royal Fort House. In conjunction with other data the outline of the fort can be suggested in more detail and precision, revealing more of the structures within it (Fig.10). Firstly there is evidence from documentary sources; secondly there is a plan published by Phillip Stainred in 1669. Thirdly there is evidence gained from field and geophysical survey.

Documentary sources for the Royal Fort

The Manor House and Cromwell House were a rebuilding of a single structure 80 feet in length which stood within the Royal Fort. In 1657 a lease to Major Harper of the house later known as the Manor House stated that it occupied 'two rooms at the south-west end in the long building there', where 'Lieutenant Mabbs lately lived'. The ground granted with the house extended to the outside of the fort ditch or 'grafte'. Later plans show the extent of the property, and enable the line of the outside of the ditch to be identified.

In 1665 the earliest lease for Cromwell House (a much later name) to John Hickes stated that his house had been lately built upon part of the foundations of a house formerly 80 feet in length. Since Cromwell House was on the same alignment as the Manor House this must have been the same structure as that upon which the Manor House was built. The lease for Cromwell House does not give any details as to whether its curtilage extended to include the fort ditch, but in 1725 the ground to the north was stated to have extended on the south to the fort ditch. The northern boundary of the land going with Cromwell House must therefore have extended to include the fort ditch. On the Ordnance Survey plan of

1884 the outline and details of the plan of the garden indicate that a bastion may have been sited here, the northern boundary of the garden taking in the ditch as it turned sharply around the point of the bastion.

Similarly the house demolished c.1760 for the present Royal Fort House was a structure dating from the military use and construction of the fort. In 1657 a lease to Mr Daniel Brereton was of 'the great house in the Royall fort wherein sometimes dwelt Captain Thomas Beale', in a renewal of the lease in 1658 stated to be 'bounded with the bulworks on the south west side & the wall on the north east be the same more or less'. The outline of the 'city ditch' is shown on a map of Cantock's Close in 1736, and the house and bulwarks are shown on Rocque's map of 1742. The outline of the bulwarks is shown on even later estate plans made before the remodelling of Tyndall's Park by Repton. The walls of the house were recorded by archaeological observation in 1985.

A fourth house within the Royal Fort was contrived out of the gatehouse, a lease of 1656 to Francis Milner, the city swordbearer, providing further evidence of the configuration of the defences. Milner's plot extended from the fort gate alongside the way into the fort to within nine feet of the doorpost of Brereton's new house, turning then in the direction of the fort ditch, then following the ditch back to a new wall extending out from the gate. The outline of the property as recorded in the early nineteenth century can be seen to follow the edge of the fort ditch and the beginnings of the bastion at the south-east corner.

Within the Royal Fort Brereton's lease of 1658 was also of a 'corner messuage', within the fort and known as the 'Court of Guard house' and 'a roome for a stable in the midst of the ranke of houses next the gate, it being now a stable'. In 1685 the rank of houses were said to be 17 yards in length. The rank of houses can now be seen as occupied by Stuart House, exactly 51 feet or 17 yards in length; the west part of Stuart House extending towards the present Royal Fort House, now the Vice-chancellor's garage, probably occupies the site of the corner or 'Court of Guard house'. With the earlier Royal Fort House some distance to the west, this would have been at the corner beyond the rank of houses extending into the fort from the gate.

Close to the corner of this rank of houses was the well for the Royal Fort. In 1645 this was 'not half finished, the water scant and troubled and far insufficient for the use of the numbers that were there'. In 1929 it was described as 'a fine well with copious spring of water and a cistern holding 10,000 gallons which till recently supplied the neighbourhood' (Parker 1929, 131).

Stainred's plan

An entirely separate source of evidence for reconstructing the Royal Fort is the map made by Philip Stainred, a teacher of mathematics in Bristol,

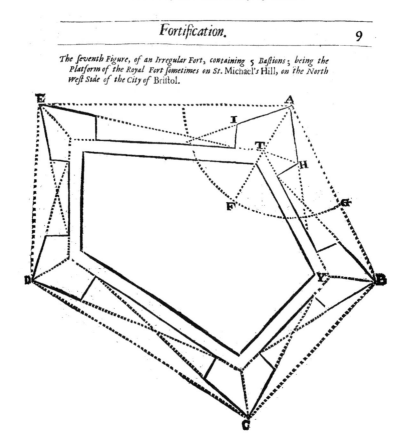

The seventh Figure, of an Irregular Fort, containing 5 Bastions; being the Platform of the Royal Fort sometimes on St. Michael's Hill, on the North west Side of the City of Bristol.

Fig 11. Stainred's plan of the Royal Fort, 1669

published as part of his treatise on the design of fortifications in Sturmy's *Mariners Magazine* in 1669 (Fig.11). The plan is entitled '... an irregular Fort, containing five bastions; being the Platform [i.e. plan] of the Royal Fort sometimes on St Michael's Hill, on the North West side of the City of Bristol'. There is no scale or compass direction. Sturmy's publication would have been known to Millerd and can be taken as the source for the plan contained in a vignette to his map of the city in 1673.

Archaeological observations

Concurrent with the preparation of this publication the mapping of the field evidence has been commenced. This has included the accurate recording of the surviving length of wall noted by Russell and the undertaking of a programme of geophysical survey, the first results of which are now available. Resistivity survey has provided a precise location for the inner edge of the fort ditch or moat on the north-west side, immediately north of the long building and the houses built upon it by Harper and Hickes, as anticipated from the documentary evidence.

Field observation also indicates that the north-west bastion or part of the rampart survives as a substantial earthwork feature, now within dense undergrowth. It can also be seen that the outer side of the fort ditch has probably determined the line taken by the road within Tyndall's Park now known as University Walk.

The reconstruction of the Royal Fort

Using these sources together a new reconstruction of the Royal Fort is now possible. First the information from the documents and from archaeological fieldwork can be combined. Secondly Stainred's unscaled and unorientated plan could be positioned over this information to achieve a best fit. Until more of the geophysics data can be studied and before more archaeological work can be undertaken, this must remain a 'best guess' as to the outline and internal arrangements of the fort. This provisional plan may usefully be compared with similar fortifications of the mid seventeenth century. The most useful analogy is to be made with the citadel on Plymouth Hoe, designed by de Gomme some twenty years later (Woodward 1987). The Royal Fort at Bristol was of a similar plan, and slightly smaller in extent, to what was first proposed by de Gomme for the Hoe. Below the lawns of Royal Fort House and adjacent buildings is the archaeology of a once formidable citadel, one of the largest single fortifications constructed by either side in the English Civil War.

The documentary sources have also revealed some of the internal arrangements of the Royal Fort. Analogies for the long barrack type buildings on the west and north-west sides can again be found in de Gomme's plans for the citadel on the Hoe. More buildings of this type possibly existed against the other inner sides of the fort walls. The rank of buildings constructed at right angles to the gate possibly formed part of a larger court, implied in the 'Court of Guard house' named in the documents.

GARDEN AND GENTRY HOUSES

Garden Houses

In the decade after the Civil War the number of houses within the area bounded by Park Row and St Michael's Hill greatly increased (Fig.12). Many of these were known as 'garden houses', a term used in 1643 by the military engineer de Gomme to describe the house formerly of George Lane in Park Row (Firth and Leslie 1925, 196). In the seventeenth century the term 'garden house' was synonymous with both 'lodge' and 'summer house'. These were terms used to describe a house which was a place of retreat from the city, a house which was seen as one with its garden. Such houses stood most often within one corner or at one side of a high walled garden. The house was best seen from the garden, or from afar. The view from the house was first of the garden and then into the distance. Such houses were emphatically different in their setting from houses built in continuous rows, such as the four houses on St Michael's Hill immediately above St Michael's church. As an addition to a residence elsewhere in the city, such houses were owned by the wealthier citizens. Most of the smaller garden houses on St Michael's Hill were owned by citizens who lived in the wealthiest city-centre parishes, notably that of St Werburgh centred on Small Street (BRO F/Tax/A/1).

At the outbreak of the Civil War one such house was that built within the garden of no. 10 Park Row. This had been called a lodge in 1548. On St Michael's Hill the small house that stood within the large garden of nos. 31–37 was similarly positioned. At least ten more 'garden houses' within this same area were specifically identified as such in the hearth tax returns for 1662. These included the garden house of Richard Gonning, later the Park Row Asylum site, one of John Hillier, probably later the site of the uphill part of Lunsford House, one of Richard Jordan, in Park Lane above the Manor House, and that of Gilbert Moore, facing St Michael's churchyard. Tower-like, these were all probably of one room on each floor. The contents of Richard Jordan's garden house were described in the inventory of his possessions made after his death in 1676. The lowest floor was a cellar for storage. Above this was a kitchen, above that a dining room, above that the best chamber, and a garret above in the roof, the inventory account matching exactly the three hearths noted in the 1662 assessment. Jordan was a painter and possessed of considerable wealth. He lived also at his house in Broad Street, a building of the mid-sixteenth century, but kept most of his possessions in what was a sumptuously furnished garden house on the hill. Pre-war photographs of a house which stood in Blackfriars below Upper Maudlin Street, rebuilt c.1990, provide the best impression of how Jordan's house might have appeared from the exterior (BRO 20894). Windows on all sides facing the garden provided distant views and underlined the courtly and tower-like qualities of the small garden house. Gilbert Moore's garden house was smaller than Jordan's, with only two hearths in 1662 being probably of just two floors. Heightened by one storey and extended outwards, Moore's garden house survived until the second world war. Two further garden houses noted in 1662 were within gardens fronting St Michael's Hill. Immediately above the row of four houses nos. 23–29 Mrs Elizabeth Cugley's garden house was probably a single storey structure, set within a large garden and probably the building shown on an early nineteenth-century plan. Several houses beyond, on the site of nos. 43–47, was the garden house of Leonard Hancocke, like Jordan's with just one hearth on each floor.

Other similarly arranged garden houses cannot certainly be identified in the 1662 hearth tax return, and some were probably built in the ensuing decades. Above the Manor House in Park Lane the garden of Richard Jordan was divided between 1695 and 1698, and a second similarly sized house was built in a second garden (no. 8 Park Lane) placed below the original house. At the north end of Stile Lane another garden house, no. 4, survived until the second world war; a detailed plan of the internal arrangements in 1807 was to be found in the title deeds for the property. Pre-war views could give the misleading impression that this was a rural cottage. In the 1690s it was the garden house of one of Bristol's wealthiest citizens, Samuel Wallis, mayor in 1696; his principal residence was in Baldwin Street. On St Michael's Hill in 1696 Wallis would have looked across the orchard, later the site of Vine Row, to what had been Jordan's garden house and which was now that of William Lewis, as sheriff another leading citizen. On the summit of St Michael's Hill the house of Eusebius Brookes, now partly surviving as Oldbury House, was initially a similar structure, built out of the gun battery at the civil war entrance to the city.

Garden or summer houses such as these continued to be built in the eighteenth century. Within the Royal Fort a drawing by James Stewart of 1752 shows in the distance the hipped roof and tower-like proportions of two summer houses, one above Royal Fort Road, the other in the garden of the house to the south of the fort gatehouse. Plans of the eighteenth century show a probably similar summer house in the gardens of Cromwell House. The still surviving red sandstone tower-like house known as Tower View was one such summer house. It is now concealed from any distant view by the new Synthetic Chemistry building. Close examination of the exterior will reveal the now blocked windows to provide more extensive vistas over Tyndall's Park and the city, and the arch which opened up the entire ground floor to the garden.

There were by the 1660s a number of garden houses which were in ground plan double the size of the above, of two rooms on each floor but similarly placed in relation to a garden surrounded by high walls. In the hearth tax return for 1662 at least two of these were considered as garden houses. Henry Jones's house with five hearths was probably the Manor House in Park Lane; Edward Tyley's garden house, now below St Michael's School, was a second such house. At least one similar house was not termed a 'garden house' by the assessors for the hearth tax. The seventeenth-century house on the south side of Old Park was in 1662 the house of Thomas Deane, possibly complementing a residence in the city centre. A number of houses similar to Deane's were built after 1662; a small part of the Strettons' house in Medical Avenue still stands above the Buildings Maintenance car parking area.

In Park Lane the Manor House was a rebuilding of c.1691 of the house shown on Millerd's map of 1673, built after 1662. Assessed for eleven hearths in 1668 it was the residence of Edward Hurne, a vintner, whose city centre property was the Mermaid Tavern in Broad Street. With its principal facade facing the garden, and with polite entry to the house only via the garden, this would have been perceived by contemporaries as a 'garden house'. On the north side of Upper Church Lane, Rupert House, so called in the nineteenth century, was built c.1674 by Richard Stubbs, a merchant whose city centre residence was in Broad Street close to Christchurch. Stubbs's residence replaced an existing lodge in a garden rented in 1548 to John Erath, a hooper. Stubbs's lease stipulated that the house was to be 'substantial', of at least two storeys and of at least two rooms on each floor. This same house survived into the age of photography, the chimneypiece dated 1674 carrying the initials of Richard Stubbs and his wife Mary. A small part of this house has now been examined archaeologically.

The greater number of the garden houses on St Michael's Hill were built within the Little Park, an estate belonging to Isaac Harper by the 1660s. Surviving leases, the earliest being two of April 7th 1660, indicate that he was actively promoting the development of his land as an estate of garden houses. Of the gentry class, Harper himself did not apparently live within the city in 1662.

Gentry houses

Surviving records from the 1660s onwards reveal that a number of houses standing within gardens were occupied by persons of gentry status. A few of these houses were similar to the garden houses so far discussed, standing at one side or in one corner of a large walled garden; the lodge at no.10 Park Row was one such example, the home of Sir William Merrick in 1696. A greater number of gentry houses stood surrounded by gardens or were more visible from the street. What such a distinction meant to contemporaries would require more research into the social backgrounds and aspirations of the inhabitants of this landscape in the later seventeenth century. The houses identifiable as garden houses were mostly occupied by wealthier citizens but not by those of gentry status. In this same period a number of the more visible and larger houses were occupied mostly by persons of gentry status, some by wealthier citizens. The greatest concentrations of such houses were on the summit of St Michael's Hill and in Park Row.

On the summit of St Michael's Hill the Royal Fort became a small estate of predominantly gentry houses initially leased by the City. Five large houses were built from c.1655 onwards. The Manor House, Cromwell House, the first Royal Fort House and the house built in part over the gatehouse each utilised existing foundations or structures. The fifth house was that built by John Garway before 1679 to the north of Royal Fort Lane. There are indications in the records of occupancy that some houses were let for short periods to different visiting gentry families. The Royal Fort offered a view, seclusion and a high status address. The unusual crenellated facades of the house to the south of the gate and of John Garway's house were possibly intended to echo the former fortress role of the location.

To the north of the Royal Fort the garden house of Eusebius Brookes was rapidly extended to become a larger house. By 1689 it had been divided to form two adjoining houses. The part closest to the city survives as Oldbury House. By the 1690s this was the home of Joseph Knight, a merchant, and his wife Lady Phillipa Gore, a marriage underlining the links between merchants and gentry. An inventory of Phillipa Gore's possessions provides a record of the arrangement and contents of Oldbury House in 1704.

A similar concentration of gentry houses was to be found in Park Row. The house once of George Lane and later of Phillip Langley and his widow was by the 1690s the house of Sir John Duddlestone and his wife. Further east the lodge at no. 10 Park Row had by 1695 been extended to form the more substantial dwelling of Sir William Merrick and his family. From c.1720 onwards this property was subdivided by George Gibbes esq. to form a small estate of six or seven houses let to persons of gentry status, Gibbes himself moving from one to another as occasion demanded. At least two further substantial dwellings had been built to the east of no. 10 Park Row by the 1690s. At no. 14 was the house of Capt. George Morgan, further east that of Sir John Knight and his family, assessed for 18 and 20 windows respectively in 1695.

A landscape occupied overwhelmingly by the wealthiest citizens and by gentry

By the early eighteenth century there were within this landscape of garden and gentry houses only a few small dwellings that might be best described as cottages, taking up much the same area of ground as a one-room plan lodge, but intended from the outset as the permanent dwellings of the less wealthy. In the Little Park, at approximately no. 16 Lower Park Hill, was the 'well house', recorded from at least 1679. Above Royal Fort Lane the house recorded from at least 1618 at the west end of Joachim's Close was of a similar size. Until c.1720 this was a landscape occupied overwhelmingly by the wealthiest citizens and by gentry.

A significant proportion of this wealth may have been generated through the trade in manufactured goods, slaves and sugar, between Bristol, Africa and the Americas. More research would be necessary to quantify the extent to which those directly involved in these trades held property within this neighbourhood in the late seventeenth and early eighteenth century. One obvious example would be Sir John Knight, the owner of extensive plantations on Nevis and one of the proprietors of the sugar refinery on St Augustine's Back. Knight lived successively in houses in Park Row and the Royal Fort.

RESIDENTIAL STREETS AND LARGER HOUSES
IN THE EIGHTEENTH CENTURY

Residential streets

Until the late seventeenth century the row of four gabled houses above St Michael's church marked the beginning of the built up area of the city, the area within which street frontages were totally occupied by buildings. The hillside above was a landscape of garden houses and gentry houses. Between 1695 and the 1720s the street frontage to the west side of the hill was gradually transformed through rebuilding and the construction of new houses (Fig.13).

Initially favoured also by the gentry as a place of residence, the west side of St Michael's Hill became a neighbourhood of moderately wealthy citizens, sea captains and widows. In the late 1690s Sir John Duddlestone was the first occupier of one of the two new houses at nos. 39–41. Its occupiers between 1707 and 1755 were Benjamin Willoughby, also a gentleman, and then his widow. Higher up the hill, no. 71 was finished about 1720. Its first occupant was John Constant, a sea captain much involved in the slave and sugar trade. Occupied by his widow from c.1736, it was briefly, in 1751–2, the home of James Stewart, writing master and historian.

In the early eighteenth century Joseph Earle, the new owner of the Little Park estate and resident in the rebuilt Manor House in Park Lane, was responsible for the development of two new residential streets, each of connected row houses. Those in Old Park Hill were possibly superior in being provided with detached brick kitchens. Old Park Hill was developed from 1714 onwards. The west part of Vine Row was commenced several years later; the east part of Vine Row was not occupied until the early 1740s. As on the west side of St Michael's Hill, these streets became favourite places of residence for sea captains and their widows. Many of the names of the former were of those active in the trade with Africa and the Americas.

Some of the new or rebuilt houses on St Michael's Hill survive; only those above the former High Park Avenue are certainly new houses of the first quarter of the eighteenth century. Lower down the hill earlier structures of the seventeenth century may be incorporated in apparently later buildings. Overall these houses may have displayed a variety of living arrangements, particularly with regard to the placement of servants and kitchens. Many houses were provided with detached kitchens, as at nos. 39 and 41 St Michael's Hill and all the houses in Old Park Hill. Here as with the houses in Vine Row, the only gardens of importance were those in front of the house, and the view of the Little Park beyond. In terms of the importance accorded to the pleasures of a private garden, these rows of residential houses were the antithesis of the garden houses which surrounded the Little Park. In Vine Row the only house with extensive gardens was the centre house, double the size of all others, and for over 30 years from 1742 the home of Thomas Jones esq. The remaining houses in Vine Row had only a small back yard, albeit with a view over Cantock's Close to the rear.

Within what was now very much a suburb of the city, wealthy citizens could from the early eighteenth century choose whether to live in one of the new row houses or to settle for an older garden house. This was a matter of individual preference. Such preferences were most clearly stated through occupation of the same house over a long period; Edward Kendrick and later his widow lived at no. 15 Vine Row from 1732 for over 40 years. John Purcell's preference was in contrast for a garden house, almost adjacent to the Kendricks' house and from 1723 his home for 35 years.

South of the Royal Fort Tinkers' Close was developed as housing for less wealthy citizens. In Royal Fort Road nos. 1–4 had been built by c.1745. A number of smaller houses, including nos. 40-44 Tinkers' Close and the four houses adjoining the distilling house, had been built by the same date. The latter were clearly in a neighbourhood less polite than streets such as Old Park Hill and Vine Row.

Before its development for housing, Tinkers' Close was possibly literally that. The rates before the mid 1730s frequently refer to the 'Tinkers' Close poor', for instance in 1733, implying the presence of residents too poor to pay. Yet, there is no evidence for any housing existing before the 1730s. Tinkers' Close was possibly an encampment of some of the poorest inhabitants of the city.

By 1828 the number of smaller houses built within existing plots had increased. In Lower Park Hill, Park Place and Upper Church Lane a number of such houses had been built since 1775. In Tinkers' Close nos. 1–7 Tyndall's Buildings or Tankard's Close were built c.1812.

Larger houses

On the summit of St Michael's Hill and in Park Row a number of the larger houses continued to be occupied by persons of gentry status throughout the eighteenth century. Most notable was the Tyndall family, responsible for the rebuilding of Royal Fort House c.1760 and the subsequent creation of Tyndall's Park. Nicholas Pocock's painting of 1785 of the Bristol quayside with the hills behind the city dominated by the new house amply summed up the nexus between the 'respectable' trade in slaves and the wealth it generated for the city's most prosperous citizens (Greenacre 1982, 5). Tyndall's Park and the landscaping of Humphrey Repton produced a new landscape of *rus in urbs*. The intricacies of the development of the Park can be best understood from Bettey's recent study (Bettey 1997, 11–15). Archaeological research could extend our knowledge of the location of the short-lived streets and houses of this failed 1790s development, possibly only partially within Tyndall's Park.

The occupants of the five or six houses at Royal Fort were for the greater part of the eighteenth century drawn from the social circle with which the Tyndalls would have comfortably mingled. Prominent amongst these in the earlier eighteenth century was Thomas Elbridge, Deputy-controller of Customs in the city, the founder of a school in Royal Fort Lane and occupier of the house extending south from the gatehouse (Bettey 1997; Elbridge's residence can now be accurately located).

In Park Row a number of the larger residences were similarly occupied by individuals whose wealth was closely related to the profits to be gained from the Atlantic trade. No. 14 Park Row was the home from 1729 to 1762 of the merchant Joseph Percival, his wealth at his death in 1762 valued at the then staggering sum of £70,000. The adjacent house no. 15, Lunsford House, was from 1766 the home of the merchant James Ireland, member of a family similarly closely connected to the Atlantic trade.

Other large houses on the summit of St Michael's Hill and in Park Row came to be occupied by persons whose wealth was built more immediately upon industry and a particular trade. On the opposite side of St Michael's Hill, St Michael's Hill House was built c.1732 by Richard Goeing, a pewterer. No. 121, Oldbury House, was from 1729 occupied by Edward Bisdee, a baker. At no. 17 Park Row the garden house of Sir Robert Gonning and Lady North became in the 1760s and 70s the home of Rowland Williams, a sugar baker, but similarly tied to the fortunes of the Atlantic trade.

Postscript

The subsequent history of the landscape of the St Michael's Hill precinct has been studied here principally as a means of understanding land use and change in the medieval and early modern period. The nineteenth- and twentieth-century maps are for instance a source of much information for earlier periods. Entirely beyond the scope of this study has been the detailed research into land use and property holdings from the late eighteenth century onwards, a subject already in part covered by Bettey (1997). The documentary sources available in the University and elsewhere in Bristol offer much scope for research into the neighbourhoods and institutions that occupied the St Michael's Hill precinct in the period up to and since the end of the Second World War.

PROPERTY AND TENEMENT HISTORIES

1. BARTHOLOMEW CLOSE, PUCKINGROVE
AND KING'S ORCHARD

Four closes, Bartholomew Close, Hither Puckingrove, Inner Puckingrove
and King's Orchard, formed a contiguous block of land parcels adjacent to
the boundary between the city of Bristol and Clifton (Figs.9–12).
Bartholomew Close and Puckingrove were thus first mentioned in the
charter of 1373 which delineated the boundaries of the new county of
Bristol.

Bartholomew Close, formerly part of the Bartholomew lands
In 1373 this was probably the field called 'Bartholomeu is clos', adjacent to
and therefore distinct from 'Fockynggrove' (BRS 1, 154–5). In 1791,
reciting a seventeenth-century description, this was the ground of – Gainer
widow (abuttals from Hither Pucking Grove).

Hither Pucking Grove, formerly part of the Bartholomew lands
In 1373 this was part of the close known as 'Fockynggrove' (BRS 1,
154–5). By 1634 it was part of Pucking Grove, held by Anthony Hodges, a
fee farm rent of £4 payable for this and other land to the Bartholomew
Lands, the lands of the former hospital of St Bartholomew now belonging
to the Grammar School (Sampson 1912, 77). In 1791 one half of this rent
was payable out of Hither Pucking Grove (University Deeds 22). The
location of Puckingrove Hither or Hither Puckingrove is shown on a plan
of 1785; this formed the basis for a similar plan of 1792, and with some
amendments was used for an abstract of title to the Tyndall lands in 1876
(Bettey 1997, 10; DC/E/3/4 fol.137; University Deeds 22). Before 1763
this had formed part of the lands of James Saunders. It was described in
1791 as being formerly of Peregrine Panton, since of Ralph Peacock
cooper and since then of Thomas Tyndall, as being bounded on the east by
Cantock's Closes, on the west by a ground of – Gainer widow, on the north
by Inner Pucking Grove, and on the south by land formerly of Anthony
Hodges (University Deeds 22).

Inner Pucking Grove, formerly part of the Bartholomew lands
In 1373 this was part of the close known as 'Fockynggrove' (BRS 1, 154–5). By 1634 it was part of Pucking Grove, held by Anthony Hodges, a fee farm rent of £4 payable to the Bartholomew Lands, the lands of the former hospital of St Bartholomew now belonging to the Grammar School (Sampson 1912, 77). In 1791 one half of this rent was payable out of Inner Pucking Grove (University Deeds 22). The location of Puckingrove Inner or Inner Puckingrove is shown on a plan of 1785; this formed the basis for a similar plan of 1792, and with some amendments was used for an abstract of title to the Tyndall lands in 1876 (Bettey 1997, 10; DC/E/3/4 fol.137; University Deeds 22). In 1785 this was described as a close of meadow or pasture, formerly in the possession of Thomas Bidwell baker, after of William Jones merchant, and then of Thomas Tyndall, sold by Naomi Dolman to Tyndall in 1785 (University Deeds 22).

The King's Orchard, property of the Corporation
In 1289–90 this was the garden which belonged to Christine the clerk (BRS 34, 24), by the early fifteenth century known as 'the king's garden on St Michael's Hill, formerly of Cristine the clerk, now of John Hobbes (GRB 1, 74; the annual rent was 18s). It became part of the lands of the Corporation through its purchase of the Royal Farm in 1462 (BRS 21, 55).

In 1684 this was the close of pasture leased to John Jones mariner, bounded on the south and south-west by the road from Bristol to Clifton and on the west and north-west by Puckingrove, by c.1700 held by Joseph

Fig 14. King's Orchard, blocked doorway in the boundary wall

Fowle, late in the possession of William Sperring, now in the possession of Peregrine Panton, leased from 1719 to Mr Joseph Fowles (04335(9) fol.176; 04238 fol.28). By 1764 the close was held by William Tappy gardener, now leased to Thomas Tyndall esq. (01010(1)).

Part of the boundary wall of King's Orchard survives to the south-west of Woodland Road. Within this length of wall is a two-centred arched doorway of the eighteenth century providing access from Cantock's Close into King's Orchard (Fig.14). To the west of this doorway is a blocked ashlar oval window or opening.

2. CANTOCK'S CLOSE

Cantock's Close occupied a considerable part of what is now the University Precinct, its name preserved in the road leading to the Chemistry Department (Figs.9–12). The de Cantock or Quantock family were members of Bristol's ruling élite by the later thirteenth century. Their ownership of the land on St Michael's Hill can be first identified in the mid fourteenth century; at his demise in the Black Death of 1349 Roger de Cantock held four enclosures on the hill, known as Cantock's Closes, passing after his death into the possession of St Augustine's Abbey (Bettey 1997, 2, for further references). Cantokkesclos' was certainly a possession of the abbey of St Augustine's by 1428; by 1491 the abbey received an annual rent of 36s from the pasture called 'Cantockesclose' (BRS 9, 35, 94–5).

In 1602 these were the three closes of pasture, known as Cantock's Closes, and one messuage newly built there by John Jones, leased to Robert Watson gent., then assigned to George Baldwin. The latter surrendered his title a year later, a new lease being granted to Mary Langley, the closes of meadow and pasture by estimation 24 acres. These and the house built by Jones were now held by George Lane, merchant (DC/E/1/1 (a) fols.15, 23, 27, 87).

In 1619 Cantocke's Close was described as being in three parts. The first was adjacent to the house and about eight acres; the second was meadow, bounded by the 'foaking grove' on the west, by the city's 'meere stones' (boundary stones) on the north, and by Sir Charles Garret's land on the east, eleven acres in all. The third was of seven acres, to the east of the first close, bounded on the north by Windmill Close belonging to the city, on the east by Tinkers' Close belonging to Sir Charles Garrett. The northern part can be seen on the plan of 1736 and on Rocque's map of 1742; the two closes to the south may have been radically changed after the taking of part of the close for the building of the Royal Fort, land that was not apparently returned after the Civil War (DC/E/3/1; DC/E/40/9 52130). The close remained in the holding of the Langley family to the early eighteenth

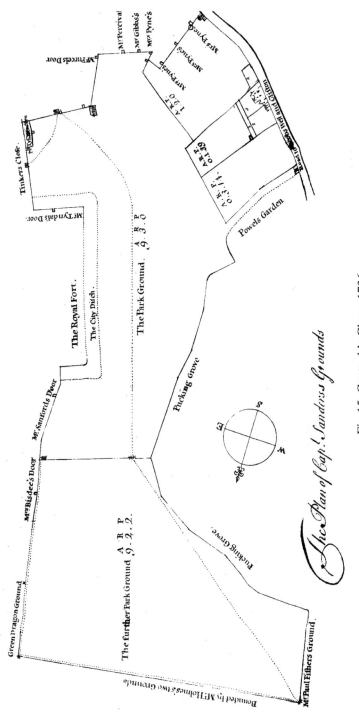

Fig 15. Cantock's Close, 1736

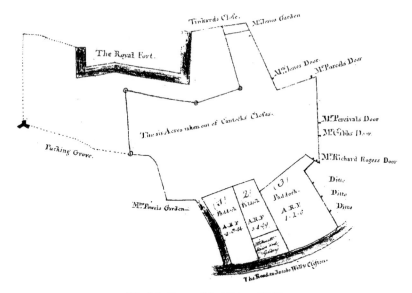

Fig 16. Cantock's Close, 1743

century, new leases being granted to Philip Langley in 1622 and to John Langley of Gloucester in 1666 (DC/E/3/2 fol.95). Philip Langley lived here in 1662, being assessed for five hearths (F/Tax/A/1).

From 1736 the close and house were leased to Mr James Saunders of London, mariner, and then from 1742 to Thomas Tyndall (Figs.15–16). The plan of the close in 1736 shows doors in the boundary on the east side belonging to Mrs Bisdee (see entry for Oldbury House, no. 121 St Michael's Hill), Mr Sanford, for the land behind the Manor House, and Mr Tyndall (DC/E/40/9 52130). Doors at the south-east end of the close belonged to Mrs Pyne (no. 29 Park Row), Mr Gibbs (no. 11 Park Row), Mr Percival (no. 14 Park Row) and Mr Purcel (nos. 2/3 Stile Lane). The same doors are shown on a plan of 1743, Mrs Pyne's door now of Mr Richard Rogers and two new doors to the east of Mr Jones (no. 9/10 Vine Row).

In a renewal of Tyndall's lease in 1767 the house late of James Stewart and then of the widow Hawkins was said to be now 'pulled down and erased', the walls of the adjacent three paddocks 'pulled down and the said three paddocks thrown into the close' (DC/E/40/48 52127–521344, the leases of 1736 and 1767 with plans endorsed; see also Bettey 1997). In their place was a gateway with a lodge on each side, newly built by Thomas Tyndall as an entrance to his park, shown on a plan of 1785 (Fig.17, from University Deeds 22). The close remained part of Tyndall's park until c.1791, when work commenced to 'form a regular and grand plan of Buildings which would be an ornament to and very much improve'

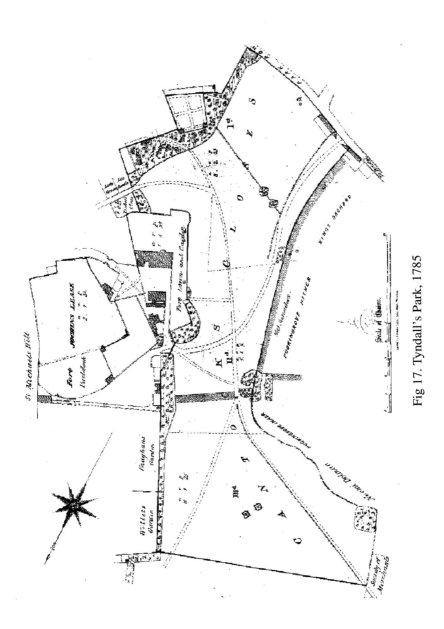

Fig 17. Tyndall's Park, 1785

the city. Together with 54 acres of adjoining land, the grounds were then laid out 'for building thereon a Crescent, Square, Circus, several Streets and other Buildings upon a regular plan ... approved by the ... Dean and Chapter' (University Deeds 22). Building within the park had not proceeded greatly before the boom in house construction collapsed in 1792. Ultimately Humphrey Repton was commissioned to redesign the landscape as visible from Royal Fort House. This work was completed by 1805, when the before and after views of the garden at Royal Fort were used by Repton to illustrate his *Observations on the Theory and Practice of Landscape Gardening* (Bettey 1997, 14–15, for references and a fuller account).

John Jones's house (demolished)

The house built by John Jones is described in the inventory of George Lane's possessions, made in 1613. Lane's principal residence was in St Werburgh's parish, probably in Small Street. The house in Cantock's Close was identified by the appraisers as 'the house att the hill' and was where he died. The rooms of the house included the upper lofts, the parlour and chambers, and the kitchen and lower rooms. The list of Lane's possessions shows that the house and adjoining 24 acres were both a farm and a place of retreat. To the former belonged three bee hives, tools for hay making and cheese making, 18 milk pans, a bull, 11 cows, 5 pigs and 28 sheep. To the

Fig 18. John Jones's house, James Stewart's in 1746

Fig 19. James Stewart's garden in 1746

latter belonged pictures, Venetian drinking glasses, a lute with its case, a drawing box, hamper and an undisclosed number of books.

There are at least five illustrations of Jones's house. Millerd's map of 1673 and an estate plan of 1736 show the house in iconographical form. The house is shown also on the Bucks' view of the city from the north-west in 1733. Two drawings by the writing master James Stewart who lived there from 1730 to 1748 depict it in consummate detail, viewed both from Park Row and from Stewart's own garden (Bodleian Library, Western MSS, Gough Somerset 2, fols.3, 5).

Occupancy from the ratebooks:
1662 Phillip Langley, five hearths, 1673 widow Langley, six hearths, 1689 widow Hurtnell, 1695 Sir John Duddlestone 13 windows, 1696 for house and Cantock's Close, but note that his residence was in St Werburgh's parish, 1711 John Taunton, 1718 widow Taunton, 1730 James Stewart (who moved to no. 71 St Michael's Hill in 1749), 1748 Jane Hawkins, 1764 onwards only a stable is mentioned here.

3. JOACHIM'S CLOSE,
SITE OF THE CHILDREN'S HOSPITAL

An undated sixteenth-century rental refers to 'Thomas Joachym's close of grounde at Michaell Hill', possibly the origin of its name; by this date it was in the occupation of Mr George Snygge. By 1581 Joachim's Close had been leased by the Dean and Chapter to Elizabeth Dee. It was then described as the remnant of a toft and 'an closse of pasture', bounded by Broome Hay on the south, by Cantock's Close on the west, by lands formerly of the nunnery of St Mary Magdalene on the north, and by the highway, now St Michael's Hill, on the east; the toft was then late occupied by Walter Pykes draper decd. From 1611 the close and toft were leased to George Snygge, now one of the barons of the Exchequer (DC/E/1/1(c) fols.107 and 141). At an earlier date the close must have formed part of the possessions of St Augustine's Abbey (Figs.9–11).

The boundaries of Joachims' Close were described in a survey of the Dean and Chapter's lands made in c.1618, starting at 'an house 40 foote long built within a stump of an house without [h]is covering [i.e. roof] 7 yards long'. The land which went with the house extended 15 yards down towards Tinkers' Close, then extending westwards to a meer stone [a boundary stone] in a bank. From here the boundary turned northwards alongside a quirk or oak [quercus] hedge separating Joachim's Close from Wimble Close, the latter probably the same as Windmill Close. At the north-west end the Dean and Chapter's land actually extended into Wimble Close 'where sometyme there was a wall dividing it from Wimble Closse' (DC/E/3/1). The house described in the c.1618 survey appears to have been at the north-west corner of the close.

By 1649 the closes 'called Joachims Closes', in the tenure of Thomas Hodges, were 'now for the most part turned into Bull workes called the Royall Fort' (DC/E/3/2 fol.101). Following the Restoration Joachim's Close again became part of the lands of the Dean and Chapter. As with Cantock's Close to the west, the part occupied by the Royal Fort seems to have now been retained as the land of the Corporation.

44

From 1662 it was leased to Thomas Hickes (DC/E/1/2 fol.141), a wealthy mercer who also held the adjacent property, Cromwell House, from the City by a lease of the same year. New leases were granted to Thomas Hickes in 1683 and to Mrs Hannah Hickes in 1713. From 1738 Joachim's Close was leased to John Elbridge esq, the owner of Royal Fort House (DC/E/40/25).

The later eighteenth-century arrangements of the gardens now occupying Joachim's Close are shown on the plan of Tyndall's lands in 1783. This shows areas of lawns with paths and green houses. Part of Joachim's Close was to the north of these gardens, shown on Fig.10 as being to the north of the boundary wall and separately named also there as Joachim's Close, a pond evidently serving as an ornamental feature close to St Michael's Hill. This northern part of Joachim's Close formed part of a larger field extending beyond the site. The southern part of Joachim's Close remained a possession of the Tyndall family until it was granted by them for the purposes of a Children's Hospital in 1881. The northern part of Joachim's Close became part of the Children's Hospital only between 1901 and 1906. The boundary wall between the two parts of Joachim's Close shown on the 1783 plan was thus perpetuated in the layout of the buildings of the hospital.

Ivy Cottage (demolished)

The 'remnant of a toft' described in more detail in the survey of c.1618 (see above) was by 1683 the little tenement of John Millard, by 1699 of Margaret Gilbert widow, as tenant to Thomas Hickes. This little tenement is shown on Rocque's map of 1742; on Stewart's two drawings of the houses at Royal Fort in 1752 it is shown as either ruinous or as being rebuilt. In 1753 there was a stable adjacent and a coach house opposite. This house was by 1881 known as Ivy Cottage (UBHT deeds with Osborne Clarke, packet 8153).

Ivy Cottage was adjacent to the much larger house belonging to the city, of Mr John Garroway in 1679, but was held by the owners of Cromwell House to the north, always part of the lease from the Dean and Chapter.

Adjacent to Ivy Cottage was the still surviving monumental brick archway of the eighteenth century (Fig.20). This was the entrance to a garden which formed part of the holdings associated with Cromwell House (DC/E/40/25).

Ivy Cottage was aligned pre-cisely on the

Fig 20. Gate formerly adjacent to Ivy Cottage

curtain wall of the fort but within it, and was possibly a structure belonging to the period of the fort, subsequently converted to a private house.

Occupancy from the ratebooks:
1698 [one of] 'Thomas Hickes for 3 tenements', 1705 Madam Hickes's small tenement in the Fort, 1710 George Woolvin for Madam Hickes's' tenement, 1711 void, 1712 [George Hacker and] William Bond in Mrs Hannah Hickes's houses, 1713 William Bond, 1714 William Bond now George Merryweather (Welthan Atwood in land tax), 1717 widow Merryweather, 1727 Richard Parsons.

George Corner's house (demolished)

A little tenement or dwelling house now of George Corner gardener, at the east end of the close, is first mentioned in 1727. It is not mentioned in a lease of 1699, but could be one of the buildings shown on the 1673 map at the south-east end of the close, at the junction of Royal Fort Lane and St Michael's Hill. The house was by 1753 'sometime since' of George Corner, and was distinct from the newly built tenement and school house (DC/E/40/25).

Occupancy from the ratebooks:
1696 Joseph Plevey, household listed, 1698 Joseph Plevy [possible inventory of 1702] in one of Mr Hickes's tenements and Thomas Hickes for three tenements, 1703 widow Hickes' 3 tattered tenements, 1705 Michael Quintin for Mrs Hickes' ten, 1706 Hacker late Quinton, 1707 George Hacker, 1712 George Hacker [and William Bond] in Mrs Hannah

Fig 21. John Elbridge's school, James Stewart, 1747

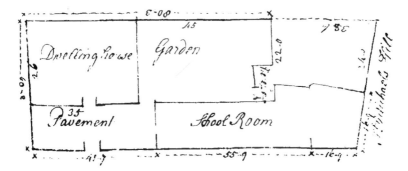

Fig 22. John Elbridge's school, plan of 1767

Hickes's houses, 1716 widow Hacker, 1719 George Corner, 1746 George Corner void.

The school (demolished)

John Elbridge died in February 1739 leaving a substantial endowment in his will for the foundation of a school for 24 girls. Situated at the corner of Royal Fort Lane and St Michael's Hill, this had been built by 1747 when illustrated by James Stewart, noted by him as the Mansion House and Charity School for Girls (DC/E/40/25; see also Bettey 1997 for a fuller account; Bodleian Library, Western MSS, Gough Somerset 2, fol.13). The plan of the school is shown on a lease of 1767 (DC/E/40/25). The site of the schoolroom must now lie within the widened Royal Fort Lane. The east end of the Faculty House must occupy the site of the Mansion House.

4. ST MICHAEL'S HILL: THE WEST SIDE NORTH OF JOACHIM'S CLOSE AND THE CHILDREN'S HOSPITAL

Rocque's map of 1742 shows a complex pattern of closes set back behind the frontages of the houses on St Michael's Hill. The history of these closes is only partially understood (Figs.9–12).

Magdalen Close

This was the ground to the north of Joachim's Close, in 1581 lands formerly of the nunnery of St Mary Magdalene (abuttals from Joachim's Close). In 1556/7 this was probably 'Mawdlen Close' on St Michael's Hill, a yearly rent of 10s now payable by Mr William Chester. By 1627 this was the close late of Mrs Snigge, known as 'Magdalen Close'; Snigge held ground to the north of Joachim's Close (BRS 24, 64 and 143; abuttals from Joachim's Close).

In 1725 this was the ground leased by the Corporation to Mary Jocham, the sister of Richard Hassell who had leased the Manor House from 1712; both the Manor House and this ground were now held by Elizabeth Harford. The ground was outside the Great Fort on the north side, bounded on the west with the ground late of Philip Langley, i.e. Cantock's Close, on the north with ground late of Mr Wise, on the east with the king's highway, i.e. St Michael's Hill, on the south with the late graft, i.e. ditch, of the fort, which ground was late held by William Atkinson as tenant to Richard Hassell (04335(10) fol.56). In 1763 this land formed part of the property purchased by Thomas Tyndall from the Corporation, its boundaries shown on a large scale plan endorsed on his conveyance (00708(1)). The same land was shown as in his ownership on the plan of the estate made in 1785 (DC/E/40/68/1).

No. 121, Oldbury House, no. 34 in 1775

Oldbury House, a modern name, was built as a suburban gentry residence in the later seventeenth century, between 1679 and 1689. It was purchased by Lady Phillipa Gore from Marmaduke Bowdler in 1692 (BCL Jefferies Colln vol. 20). The house is built in stone, now rendered, of three storeys with gables to the attic rooms, one room in depth with a projecting stair-wing to the rear. The kitchen/ ballroom block to the rear may be original to the house, or alternatively is possibly a later addition. The development of the house can be understood through surviving features, through inventories of 1704 and 1730, through its partial depiction on illustrations of the 1820s and through the record of occupancy from the ratebooks.

Occupancy from the ratebooks:
1679 no entry, 1689 Lady Gore, 1696 Joseph Knight esq. and Dame Phillipa Gore, 1703 Joseph Knight esq., 1706 Lady Gore's house and garden, 1707 the house late of Lady Gore, 1709 Richard Haynes esq., 1719 the house that Justice Haines did live in, 1722 William Williams now Edward Bisdy, 1729 Mr Bisdee, 1731 widow Bisdee, 1765 Charles Horwood, then 1773 Capt. Henry Holmes, at no. 34 in 1775.

Nos. 123–131, Eusebius Brookes's house (demolished)
A large and complex house of the seventeenth century was demolished before 1828, probably in 1823 (BRSMG M.1734–5, N.109). A stone fireplace of the seventeenth century is shown on a watercolour of 1823; to this is added a note '1683 B E E'. The house is shown in outline on Rocque's map of 1742. This house can be identified as that of Eusebius

Fig 23. Oldbury House, St Michael's Hill, in 1999

Brookes, assessed in the hearth tax of 1662 for seven hearths. In 1662 Brookes also occupied a city-centre residence in the parish of St Werburgh (F/Tax/A/1). The 'B E E ' of 1683 are Brookes, Eusebius and Elizabeth.

In 1667 Brookes was granted permission by the Corporation to fill in a deep and dangerous ditch alongside the road leading from his house towards Westbury (04335(5) fol.44). The map of 1742 shows how the road narrowed abruptly in front of Brookes's house. One possible explanation for this narrowing of the road is that Brookes's house was built on the site of the civil war battery at the entrance to the city. In the Civil War the defensive line around the city had extended north-eastwards from the Royal Fort to the 'platforme by Mile (i.e. St Michael's) Hill Gate', where there was a battery of two guns in July 1643. De Gomme wrote that here 'the line crookes a little northward to fetch in' close to the house of Alderman Jones which was 'upon the Highwaye's side'; in the siege of 1643 this house was 'more than Canon proofe, and most secure against the Enemies shot' (Russell 1995, 22). Jones's house was probably that shown on the 1742 map as furthest out from the city on the east side of St Michael's Hill, later known as Belfield House, a small part now remaining as no. 114. Brookes's house was on the opposite side of the road at exactly the point where a defensive line skirting Belfield House would have crossed the road.

The house was possibly first built as a lodge, then enlarged as a suburban gentry residence in the late seventeenth century.

Fig 24. Eusebius Brookes's house, from St Michael's Hill
(Oldbury House on left)

Fig 25. Eusebius Brookes's house, from the rear (Oldbury House on right)

Occupancy from the ratebooks:
1662, 1679, 1689 Eusebius Brookes, c.1694 Elizabeth Brookes and servant, 1696 Mr Kirke late Mr Holmes, 1698–9 widow Kirke for Mr Holmes house and ground, 1714 Mrs Young ?, 1719, 1722 Richard Jefferys, 1733 Robert Holmes, 1734 – Cox, 1736 Mrs Cox new houses, 1737 Thomas Holmes, 1744 void, 1745 Thomas Day, 1748 William Foot (for his school see Latimer, *18th Century Annals*, 242), at no. 35 in 1775.

No. 133, the Green Dragon, later the Swan, then the White Bear

The Green Dragon is first mentioned in the ratebooks for 1712. In 1732 it was described as the tenement where Eusebius Brookes gent. and then Robert Kirke merchant had lived, with an orchard, garden, stable and coach house now converted into a dwelling house known as the 'Green Dragon'. The evidence from the ratebooks indicates that the Green Dragon must have been a part of Eusebius Brookes's house; its earlier history is therefore discussed above. The White Bear is now substantially of the nineteenth century, following the demolition of Eusebius Brookes's house and the earlier White Bear, formerly the Green Dragon, in c.1823.

Occupancy from the ratebooks:
1712 Matthew Follett for the Green Dragon, 1714 Thomas Watkins, 1719 Mr Tucker at the Green Dragon, 1722 John Batten, 1725 Richard Griffin, 1730 Thomas Poole, 1731 Green Dragon void, 1732 Henry Hicks, 1737 The Green Dragon, 1738 The Swan now Thomas Williams, 1743 William

Pierce, 1744 Otto Strack, 1747 John Perrott, 1748 William Knight, 1754
Jane Bevan, 1765 William Bower (at the White Bear in 1764, ed. McGrath
and Williams 1979, 54), 1773 widow Bower, at no. 36 in 1775, 1775 John
Hewett, 1801 James Gurner.

The former paddocks behind Eusebius Brookes's house
In 1732 these were the two paddocks containing c.4 acres now converted
into garden ground, formerly in the holding of Edward Harford merchant
(AC/JS 8 (5)).

The rope walk
Cutting across the land formerly of St Bartholomew's in 1743 was a rope
walk, shown on the plan of that date as contiguous with a narrow orchard
against the city boundary. Both are shown on Rocque's map of 1742
(04479(2) fol.37).

The bowling green
Adjacent to the land formerly of St Bartholomew's in 1743 was a bowling
green, shown on the plan of that date; it is shown but not named on
Rocque's map of 1742. Adjacent to the bowling green, at the back of the
yard of the Green Dragon, was a pond (04479(2) fol.37).

Occupancy from the ratebooks:
1705 Robert Poole for Mr Holmes's land, 1706 Richard Theales (for the
bowling green 1707 onwards), 1710 William Chandler for the same.

Land formerly of St Bartholomew's Priory
In 1373 the description of the boundaries of the new county of Bristol
referred to a stone fixed at the eastern corner of a certain croft of the houses
of the religious of Magdalen and Bartholomew of Bristol; only the history of
the part belonging to the Bartholomews can be traced (BRS 1, 157). In 1634
Anthony Hodges paid an annual rent of 10s for a close of meadow on St
Michael's Hill, leased from the Bartholomew Lands in 1611. In 1702 this
was the close formerly of Anthony Hodges, after of Eusebius Brookes,
adjoining lands of Eusebius Brookes his nephew and late of Phillipa Gore,
bounded on all sides with land of Brookes, except on the west where it
bounded Cantock's Close (04335(8) fol.154). The extent and precise location
of the close is shown on plans of 1743 and 1791; these plans were made
because the croft had been joined with other closes and then divided in such a
way that the original boundaries could be recorded only by boundary stones,
in 1791 marked 'BW' for Betty Willett (04479(2) fol.37; 00568(9) b,c,f).
From 1763 the close was leased to Richard Ash (09082(2) fol.976).

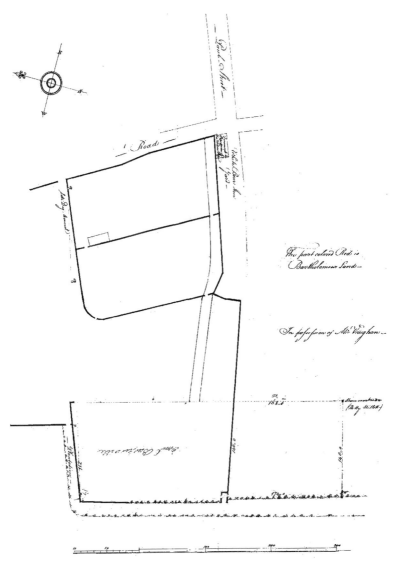

Fig 26. Bartholomew lands, as shown on plan of 1791; St Michael's Hill runs from south-east to north-west, turn 90° for correlation with Fig.13

The city boundary

Close to St Michael's Hill the location of two city boundary stones is shown on a plan of 1791 (00568(9)). These would have continued the line of 'meere stones' recorded in 1619 on the north side of Cantock's Close (see p.38), and were possibly amongst the stones marking the city's boundary as defined in 1373 (p.10).

5. THE ROYAL FORT

The Royal Fort within the Civil War period has already been discussed. This section considers the development of housing within the fort, promoted by the Corporation from 1655 onwards (Figs.10-12). Millerd's map of 1673 shows somewhat schematically the houses that had been built within the Royal Fort. Furthest west on the map was Royal Fort House (Fig.27). To the east and touching the edge of the map were the Manor House and the low and higher parts of Cromwell House, To the south were the houses to either side of the gatehouse. Millerd's map of c.1710 makes two revisions to the area immediately outside the fort, one the addition of a garden to the south-west of the gatehouse, the other the addition of a further house to the north of the gatehouse (Fig.3).

Fig 27. The Royal Fort, Millerd, 1673

Royal Fort House, no. 1 Fort in 1775
The predecessor of Royal Fort House is shown on Rocque's map of 1742, approximately at right angles to the axis of the present house. The house is shown in a probably schematic fashion on a view of St Michael's Hill, undated but c.1700, on Monamy's painting of Broad Quay in the early eighteenth century and on the two views by the Bucks of the city in 1733. The walls of the house were recorded by archaeological observation in 1985 (Russell 1995, 22).

In 1655 the Corporation agreed to lease to Daniel Brereton the 'great house in the Royall Fort – wherein Captain Beale lately dwelt, together with the garden adjoining ... and one acre of ground ... to be allotted by such person as the surveyors shall appoint ... with two shedds for wood & coales next behind the place where the court of guard was usually kept and to have the comon use of the well of water there in comon with others'. In 1657, the two sheds being removed, Brereton was given additionally 'a roome for a stable in the midst of the ranke of houses next the gate, it being now a stable' (04335(4) fol.25)). To this was added in 1658 a 'corner messuage', within the fort and known as the 'Court or Guard house', covenants obliging Brereton first not to use the property as a tavern or alehouse and secondly to vacate the corner tenement at three days notice for its use as a pest house for the city should there be an outbreak of plague (04335(4) fol.83).

In 1667 the property was leased to James Bridges the husband of Dorothy Brereton, in 1676 to Richard Corsley goldsmith, subsequently held by William Smith mariner and then by Joseph Smith merchant, before being leased in 1706 to John Grant merchant (04335(6) fol.55 and (8) fol.201). From 1717 it was leased to his widow Cecilia Grant, the part formerly assigned to Sir William Hayman by Margaret Pennington now excluded, from 1734 to Thomas Gibbs, now in the possession of Thomas Ware merchant (04335(11) fols.77 and 91). From 1737 it was leased to Thomas Tyndall merchant (04335(12) fol.7).

The history of the house as rebuilt c.1760 is much better known and need not be repeated at length here (Ison 1950; Mowl 1991). Several comments can though be usefully added in regard to these accounts.

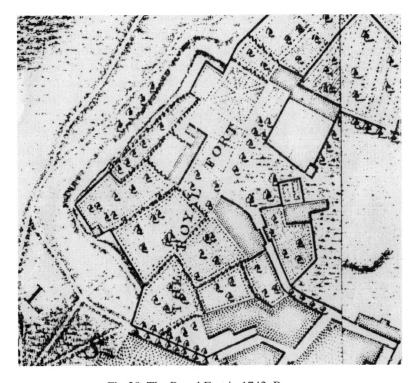

Fig 28. The Royal Fort in 1742, Rocque

There is no evidence that the Royal Fort House was 'added to an earlier house which then acted as its service area' (Mowl 1991, 86). No such house is shown on the map of 1742. The service wing to Royal Fort House is probably of the same date as the main house. Within the service part there are no features which might belong to an earlier house; rather the heavy ovolo mouldings which characterise the trim to the door and window cases can be paralleled elsewhere in Bristol in the preceding two decades as ornament to less polite spaces, for instance in the Exchange Tavern, part of the Exchange, and in the service additions made to Stoke House, Stoke Bishop (now Trinity Theological College).

Occupancy from the ratebooks:
Before 1650 Captain Beale, 1662 Daniel Britton, assessed for 10 hearths, 1668 and 1673 Jacob Bridger 10 hearths, 1679 and 1689 Thomas Biss, c.1694 widow Bisse ?, 1696 (war) Capt. William Smith for late Mr Bisse's house, 1703 (poor rate) William Smith, 1706 Mr John Grant, 1712 Mrs Saunders widow, 1713 Mr Grants late Mrs Saunders, 1714 Mr Grant, 1717 Thomas Burge, 1722 Burge now Thomas Weare, 1737 Mrs Ware, 1738 Onisopherous Tyndall, 1760 Thomas Tyndall esq., at no. 1 Fort in 1775.

The Manor House, no. 2 Fort in 1775 (demolished)
The south elevation of the Manor House, a modern name, is shown on a drawing by James Stewart of April 10th 1752 (Bodleian Library, Western MSS, Gough Somerset 2). The south and north elevations are shown on three drawings by Loxton, two of these published in 1920 (Bristol City Library, Loxton drawings; University Library, Special Collections, cuttings from the Western Daily Press, 31st January 1920).

The house was of three storeys with dormer windows to the attic rooms. By 1752 the south elevation had probably been altered through the removal of attic gables and through the insertion of sash windows; two stacks, each of three angled chimneys, remained in situ until the demolition of the house

in 1920. On the north side the original house had evidently been extended backwards with two adjoining cross-wings, probably in the early eighteenth century. Further back was a two storey range at right angles to the main house, with two mullioned and transomed windows of the seventeenth century to the ground floor.

This house was built upon or incorporated an existing

Fig 29. The 'Manor House'

THE 'OLD MANOR HOUSE, ROYAL FORT, ST MICHAEL'S HILL, FROM THE BACK

Fig 30. The 'Manor House' from the rear

structure, probably part of a barrack block built within the Royal Fort during the Civil War. In 1657 this was the property leased to Mr John Harper, the part of the house wherein Lieutenant Mabbs lately lived, containing 'two rooms in the south west end in the long building there with all the ground behind that part of the said house, extending to the outside of the Graft, and from the end of the same part of the said house, soe far as the citie land goes next adjoining to Mr Langleys ground and before the said part of the house soe far as the city surveyors have already marked the same containing by estimacion fortie foote or thereabouts', together with direct access to the well by Mr Daniel Brereton's house (04335(4) fol.60). New leases were granted to Mr John Harper gent. in 1693 and 1697 (04335(7) fol.147 and (8) fol.44), and from 1712 to Richard Hassell (04335(9) fol.1). In 1702 it was where Edward Harford lived, in 1713 where his widow now lived (abuttals from Cromwell House). From 1725 it was leased to Mary Jocham, the lease simply repeating the description in that of 1657, but now with an additional two acres of ground outside the fort on the north side, for which see under Magadalen Close above (04335(10) fol.86). In 1763 the house and ground was sold to Thomas Tyndall esq. (00708(1)). The house was demolished for new university buildings between 1920 and 1927

Occupancy from the ratebooks:
Before 1657 Lieutenant Mabbs, 1662 and 1668 John Harper, assessed for 6 hearths, 1673 for 5 hearths, 1679 John Harper, c.1694 Sir William Whetstone ?, 1695–6 Robert Clarke, 1696 Robert Clarke now Edward Harford, 1703 Edward Harford, 1705 Edward Harford for Harper's house, 1706 Haynes for Harford's house, 1707 Mr Goddard, 1708 widow Harford for Goddard's, 1709 Mrs Elizabeth Harford widow, 1714 Mrs Elizabeth Hartford now Hasell, 1714 Richard Hazell, 1729 Richard Gravett, 1733 Mr Gravat now Ld. Somerfield, 1735 Robert Sandford, 1760 Thomas Tyndall esq., 1761 void, 1762 Samuel Rich, 1766 Mrs Rich, 1772 Mrs Elizabeth Dickenson, 1775 Mrs Mary Dickenson, at no. 2 Fort in 1775.

Cromwell House, no. 3 Fort in 1775 (demolished)
The south elevation of Cromwell House, a modern name, is shown on a drawing by James Stewart of April 10th 1752 (Bodleian Library, Western MSS, Gough Somerset 2, fol.15). The north elevation is shown on a sketch

Fig 31. Low and high parts of Cromwell
House in 1752, Manor House on left

by Loxton, not dated, but of the
late nineteenth or early twentieth centuries (Bristol City
Library, Loxton drawings). No
other illustrations of the house
have yet been traced. It was
demolished between 1885 and
1903 (compare Figs.7 and 8).

Stewart's drawing shows
that closest to the Manor
House was a low structure of
one and a half storeys, with
three attic gables and a high
chimney stack at the west
end. Further west was a much
loftier house, with three attic
gables and end chimney stacks; Stewart appears to have omitted the
windows at the first floor. Loxton's drawing shows the house from the north
east (it can be correlated with the Ordnance Survey map of 1884). The main
part of the house appears to be in ruins, except possibly for a rear stair tower;
one wing to the rear was evidently of the early eighteenth century, of two
storeys with a hipped roof and probably a modillion cornice.

Cromwell House had been built by 1665, when the Corporation leased to
John Hicks, mercer, a piece of ground in 'the great forte ... where a house
formerly stood', 80 foot in length, 'upon part of which said foundation ...
John Hicks has lately erected and built a house three storeys in height
(04335(5) fol.28). The hearth tax assessment for 1668 (below) can be
interpreted as referring both to the low house next to the Manor House, of
the widow Hickes, and the lofty house to the north-west, the 'new house' of
Capt. Hickes. From 1688 the property was leased to Thomas Hicks gent.,
from 1702 to Hannah Hicks, the house now occupied by John Knight gent.
By 1713 it was the home of William Hopton esq. From 1727 it was leased
to John Elbridge, it being made clear in the lease that he was not the
occupant; this lease was renewed in 1738, and subsequently assigned to
Henry Woolnough (04335(8) fol.153, (9) fol.14, (10) fol.89, (12) fol.230).
It was leased from 1788 to John Broughton gent., from 1791 to Samuel
Edwards of Cotham House, from 1801 to Charles Ridout linen draper, from
1823 to Henry Hunt, chocolate manufacturer 09082(1) fol.395). It did not
form part of the Tyndall estate.

Occupancy from the ratebooks:
1668 widow Hickes assessed for 4 hearths, Capt. Hickes new house,
garden and stables assessed for 5 hearths, 1673 assessed for 4 hearths, 1679
alderman Hickes, 1689 Thomas Hickes, 1695–6 to 1698–9 Andrew

FitzHerbert, 1703–5 widow Hicks, 1706 Col. Henley, 1709 Mrs Hicks void, 1710 Sir William Whetstone, 1711 Lady Whetstone, 1712 Col. Hopton for the sd Mrs Hannah Hickes house where the late Sir William Whetstone inhabited, and for the ground belonging to the same, 1714 Col. Hopton, probably 1717 Richard Haines esq., certainly 1719 Richard Haines esq., 1733 Ann Haynes, 1749 Sage and Holland, 1754 James Purnell, 1772 Mrs Judith Burns, 1775 John Jones, at no. 3 Fort in 1775.

Richard Garway's house, north side of Fort Lane, no. 4 Fort in 1775 (demolished)

The south-east and north-east elevations of this house, adjacent to Ivy Cottage and Joachim's Close, are shown on two drawings by James Stewart of April 9th and 10th 1752 (Bodleian Library, Western MSS, Gough Somerset 2, fol.14). It was probably of two rooms in depth, of three storeys with a projecting two-storey porch, both this and the main house with crenellated parapets. Within the garden was a summer house, probably of a single storey, and with a pyramidical roof. A late eighteenth-century plan shows the house, the extent of the garden, the court behind and the coach house and stable, the

Fig 32. Richard Garway's house, 1752

last shown on Stewart's drawings. Stewart's two drawings disagree on the number of windows on the second floor. By 1884, shown on the Ordnance Survey map as the Preventive Home for Girls, the house had been much extended; no photographs have been traced.

A house and garden here was held by John Garway by 1679; it was probably built after 1673, being shown as an addition on the revised Millerd's map of c.1710 (F/Tax/A/1/4). In 1685 and 1695 this was the property leased by the Corporation to Sir William Merrick, for Sir William Hayman, consisting of a tenement lately built by John Garway and now in the tenure of John Yeamans (04335(8) fol.17). By 1712 it was held by Richard Gravatt book seller (04335(8) fol.292). From 1714 it was occupied by Elizabeth Galbraith (see ratebooks). It was leased to her from 1740; an earlier lease could not be traced (04335(12) fol.79). From 1787 it was leased to Edward Bowles esq., from 1798 to the Revd. Thomas Biddulph, from 1840 to Sir George Grey, from 1862 to Christopher Goodwin. Its position can be precisely located (04043(4) fol.278 annotated 'NR 397'; 04479(3) fol.61; 09082(1) fol.397).

Occupancy from the ratebooks:
1679, 1689 John Garway, 1694–1705 John Yeamans, 1705 Lady Hayman's house void, 1706 Edward Tibbett, ditto 1707 and 1709, John Jones esq. for Mr Gravett void, 1714 Mrs Galbraith at Mr Gravet's house, 1714 Mrs Elizabeth Galbraith, 1745 William Thornhill, void, 1749 Samuel Newman, 1754 Robert Croome, void, 1760 Richard Cox esq., 1770 Mr Edward Bowles, at no. 4 Fort in 1775.

The fort gate and house to the south, no. 5 Fort in 1775, later no. 9 Royal Fort Road (part demolished)
The south-east elevations of this house are shown on two drawings by James Stewart of April 9th and 10th 1752 (Bodleian Library, Western MSS, Gough Somerset 2, fol.15). The part closest to the gate, probably oversailing it, was of four storeys with attic gables and end chimney stacks, this part of the house being two rooms wide including the gateway. The further part was of two loftier storeys, with string courses, a projecting porch and crenellated parapet; this design matched closely that of John Garway's house. This house, much altered or rebuilt, was partially destroyed during the second world war (Aerofilms A21237; Winstone 1950-1953 (127); Winstone 1961 (122) is a more useful view of the rear).

In 1656 this was the gatehouse and void ground adjoining, in all about one quarter of an acre, leased to Francis Milner, sword bearer to the Corporation. The plot extended from the fort gate along by the way on the north side up to the new built house of Mr Daniel Brereton, nine foot from

his door post, and then by the same wall on the west part [i.e. of the house] to the end thereof, and from thence on the west side along by Mr Wild's ground to the graft or fort ditch, and so along by the same ditch or graft to the way leading to the new wall adjoining to the fort gate on the east side (04335(4) fol.81). New leases describing

Fig 33. House to south of gate, 1752

the property in similar terms were granted to Sarah Seward widow in 1681, to James Seward in 1682, and to Elizabeth Harford in 1714 (04335(7) fols.5 and 21, (9) fol.19). By 1740 the property was held by Elizabeth Harford. Its position can be precisely located (04043(4) fol.278 annotated 'NR 396'; 04479(3) fol.61).

The inventory of John Elbridge's possessions made after his death in 1738 show that this was a richly furnished house. The inventory lists *inter alia* the books in his library, the contents of his laundry, the room adjacent, green room, red room, red tapestry room, green tapestry room, little parlour, hall and stairs, and chambers above. Some of these may have been within what is now Stuart House (see below). Separate were a brewhouse and summer house, the latter shown on one of Stewart's drawings.

From 1782 it was leased to Thomas Bonville rope maker, who by 1787 had rebuilt 'the greater part' of the tenement and gatehouse, now assigning his lease to William Dyer apothecary (University Deeds 132). By 1791 it was held by the Revd. Samuel Seyer, from 1814 held by Messrs Biddulph and Palmer, from 1825 leased to George Downing Bowles, from 1859 leased to Edward Bowles Fripp, sold to Messrs. Wills in 1917 (09082(1) fol.396).

Occupancy from the ratebooks:
1668 the gatehouse, one hearth, 1689 James Seward and ground, 1694 James Seward, 1695–6 and 1696 George Morgan gent., 1698–9 John Knight for a house, garden and stable, 1703 Sir John Knight, 1705 void, 1705–1707 Madam Pope, 1709 Mr Coisgarne, 1714 Mr Coisgarne now Mrs Harford, 1717 Mrs Harford, 1719 John Elbridge esq., 1740 – Crisp, 1745 David Dehany, void, 1749 Edward Harford, at no. 5 Fort in 1775.

The garden ground held with the above, later nos. 7–9 Royal Fort Road

In 1654 this was the garden ground of about half a quarter of an acre on the east side of the Great Fort, together with one 'anciently built' tenement at its south-east end, leased by the Corporation to John Street yeoman, with a covenant to undertake reparations within two years (04335(4) fol.14).

In 1732 this was the orchard adjacent to Tinkards Close, formerly of James Seward merchant, but now of Elizabeth Harford widow or of her undertenant John Elbridge esq., sold by Thomas Holmes to Henry Woolnough gent. (AC/JS 8(5)). From 1782 it was leased to Thomas Bonville ropemaker, a plan said to be shown on a lease of that date (University Deeds 132). The lease of 1782 cannot now be found; the plan is almost certainly the same as that of 1781 retained by the Corporation (04479(1) fol.201a).

In 1816 no. 6 was the house lately built by John Irving merchant (abuttals from no. 5 Royal Fort Road). In 1870 this was said to be formerly occupied by John Irving (University Deeds 260).

Stuart House, not separately identified in 1775

The main part of Stuart House or its predecessor was in 1657 the 'ranke of houses next the gate', one part in the middle now a stable belonging to Royal Fort House (04335(4) fol.25)). Next to it in 1658 was a 'corner messuage', within the fort and known as the 'Court or Guard house', covenants obliging Brereton, the owner of Royal Fort House not to use the property as a tavern or alehouse and to vacate the corner tenement at three days notice for its use as a pest house for the city should there be an outbreak of plague (04335(4) fol.83).

In 1685 and 1695 this was the property leased together with John Garway's house (see above) by the Corporation to Sir William Merrick, for Sir William Hayman, a corner messuage formerly called 'the court of a Guard House with the roome or building in the midst of the rank of houses and buildings near the gate there and lately used as a stable and also in the woodhouse between the said corner tenement & late stable all containing in length in the said rank of buildings seaventeen yards or thereabouts', part of the property leased to Richard Corsley in 1676. By 1695 the last were two tenements held by George Ellis and –, and a stable held by John Yeamans (04335(8) fol.17). By 1712 the corner messuage, rooms and stable had been converted into two houses and a stable, now occupied by George Ellis gent. and John Yeamans merchant (04335(8) fol.292).

Probably by 1738 and certainly by 1781 it was leased with and was part of the house extending southwards from the gatehouse. In 1738 some of the rooms recorded in Elbridge's inventory would therefore have been within Stuart House or its predecessor (see above). Records of separate occupancy (see below) cease c.1716; this is probably when it became part of the house over and next to the gatehouse. Plans of 1781 and of 1803 show the two houses as one property (04479(1) fols.201a and b). Between these dates it was probably rebuilt, being extended southwards to become approximately double its former width. The plan of 1781 shows the well immediately beyond the north-west corner of Stuart House, the well of the fort, not completely finished when Prince Rupert surrendered in 1645 (Russell 1995, 22).

Stuart House is described in the official lists as being of the early nineteenth century and in the late Georgian style. It is certainly now heavily restored and much altered following building works c.1984 (University of Bristol, Office of the Bursar, drawing no. 200/295).

Parts of the structure correspond exactly to the walls shown in outline on the 1781 plan. These may be of the seventeenth century and of Civil War date, the only such structures to survive above ground within the Royal Fort. The vice-chancellor's garage is possibly the 'corner messuage' known in 1658 as the 'Court or Guard house'. The main part of Stuart House could incorporate masonry of the same date.

Occupancy before 1716 from the ratebooks:

1. 1696 George Ellis, household listed, 1698 George Ellis, 1705 widow Ellis for a tenement of Lady Hayman's, 1710 Samuel Yeamans, 1712 Mary Tracy, 1715 Thomas Cole, 1716 no entry.
2. 1696 Roger Buxton, household listed, 1698 Edward Jones, 1705 Samuel Evans for a tenement of Lady Hayman's, 1707 John Crease, 1716 no entry.

For after 1716 see no. 5 Fort, the gatehouse and house to the south.

6. TINKERS' CLOSE, LATER TANKARD'S CLOSE

Tinkers' Close was subdivided and sold in separate parts from 1683 onwards (Figs.11–12):

The land leased to William Rufford, site of nos. 53–57 St Michael's Hill
In 1683 this was the paddock enclosed by a dry stone wall, containing one third of an acre, leased by Eusebius Brookes to William Rufford, part of his close called 'Tinkers' Close', adjoining to St Michael's Hill, on the lower side adjoining to the dwelling house and land owned by Brookes, but in the possession of Roger Buckstone, bounded on all other sides by lands belonging to Brookes. Rufford covenanted to build a stone dwelling house within one year, and another good dwelling or summer house within three years. From 1690 an annual rent of £7 was payable to the parish of St Michael through the gift of Eusebius Brookes, later made up of sums of £1, £5 and £1, payable for an inclosed garden belonging to the house built by James Seward, for Tinkard's Close by Seward's tenants and for the houses by William Russell built thereon (Manchee 1831, 1, 133).

No. 53 St Michael's Hill, with lower garden to the rear
No. 53 was probably the first of the houses to be built by William Rufford on the plot leased by Eusebius Brookes in 1683. Although described in the statutory lists as being of the early nineteenth century, this house is substantially as built in the late seventeenth century, of three storeys with a cellar below. Ceiling beams on the ground and first floors and the stairs are all of the late seventeenth century.

Occupancy from the ratebooks:
1689 not void but occupant not listed, 1695 Samuel Payne, assessed for 8 windows, 1696 household listed, 1698–1707 John Beacher (but 1700 Joseph Smith), 1709 John Beacher void, 1712–1717 Mr Isaac Crumpe, 1718 Capt. Wheeler, 1719 Capt. Joseph Thomas, 1739 John Hale, 1755 Mrs Hale, 1775 Miss Hale, no. 25 in 1775 (note that John, then Ann then

Sarah Hale successively held the lower garden to the rear, no. 39 Tankards Close).

Nos. 55 and 57 St Michael's Hill (demolished)
Two houses had been built by 1698 or earlier on the ground leased to William Rufford (see below); their occupants are first noted from 1703. The two houses demolished in the 1950s were probably of the early eighteenth century, with later doorways (University Library, Special Collections).

Fig 34. Nos. 53–57 St Michael's Hill

Occupancy from the ratebooks:
1689 two houses void, 1695 William Ruffet 7 windows, 1698 William Rufford two tenements, 1705–1707 Daniel Pill, 1709 Daniel Pill's two houses, also:

No. 55:
1703– Mouncy, 1705 Thomas Mayne for Sandford's house, 1706 John Hicks for Sandford's, 1707–1709 Samuel Yeamans, 1712 Margaret Bayly widow, 1713 Margaret Baily now William Rickets, 1714–1718 William Ricketts, 1719 William Nicholls, 1722 widow Hacker now Mrs Sandford's, 1733 Capt. Collis, 1745 Mrs Stubbs, 1759 Mrs Marklowe, 1775 Miss Marklove, no. 26 in 1775.

No. 57:
1705 Daniel Pill, 'a house yt is building', 1712 Capt. Coward for Mr Daniel Pill's house, 1713–1714 Capt. Richard Coward, 1717 Samuel Jones, 1718 Samuel Jones now Stephens, 1719 Capt. Stevens, 1722 Mr Holmes, 1733 Mr Holmes now Taylor, 1735 Mr Hale, 1740 Thomas Tomlinson, 1745 Nathaniel Nangle, 1749 Mrs Dolman, 1755 Mrs Mitchell, 1759 Mrs Bailey, no. 27 in 1775.

Robert Holmes's development, nos. 59–71 St Michael's Hill, built 1712–1726
Above William Rufford's development and the way into Tinkers' Close, the frontage of St Michael's was developed by Robert Holmes from 1704 onwards. The first house to be built on the street front was no. 59, occupied by 1712 and demolished in the 1950s. On the plot above, no. 61/3 was built on the plot leased by Robert Holmes to Betty Hollister in 1722, 34ft wide

Fig 35. No. 59 St Michael's Hill

on the street and 31ft wide at the rear, a house of John Crosby on the south. The house built on this plot was 'lately erected' in 1726. In the nineteenth century no. 61/3 was divided (University Deeds 118; abuttals from no. 65).

Further up the hill nos. 69 and 71 were occupied by 1721, leaving a gap in the centre of the row. No. 69 was totally rebuilt internally in the 1950s. No. 71 was in the same period converted into flats and the original stairs removed; one room on the ground floor retains most of the original full height panelling.

Nos. 65 and 67 were built in the gap on the plot granted to Captain Joseph Barnes in 1726. He was to build one or more substantial dwelling houses 'of three stories high' expending at least £100; the builder was probably George Tully (University Deeds 102). Externally the two houses were clearly built as a pair, each of three full storeys with an attics and with cellars below. No. 65 was rebuilt internally in the early nineteenth century. No. 67 retains the original exterior doorcase with shell hood and internally the staircase and much of the interior trim, including a fully panelled entrance and stairs hall.

Several houses were also built at the backs of these plots (see nos. 37 and 38 Tankard's Close). The first lease to be granted in 1704 to Charles Fleetwood was possibly of a house facing into Tinkers' Close. The ratebooks show that two houses were occupied here from 1712 (see nos. 37 and 38 Tankard's Close below). At the rear of no. 59, nos. 34–6 Tankard's Close were certainly built by the 1790s (see below). To the rear of no. 67 a summer house had been built by 1754 at the west end of the garden then occupied by John Wade gent. (University Deeds 102).

Occupancy from the ratebooks:

A. 1709 no entry, 1712–1714 Mr Thomas Summers, 1717 Summers now Mrs Huffolman, 1718 widow Sumers, 1719 probably Mr Perryman, 1722 James Tudor now Clack; 1733 Mr Saunders now Bolster, 1735 Dr Swaile, 1740 Jeremiah Swale void, 1745 David Crone, 1749 Capt. Punter, 1754 Madam Bray or Capt. Punter, 1759 Capt. Punter, 1770 Mrs Punter's, 1775 William Holbrook.

B. 1709 no entry, 1712–1719 Samuel Tedder, 1722 Capt Thomas Stephens, 1733 now Sommers, 1736 Mr Pritchett, 1741 Richard Williams now Hale, 1745 Richard Bidmead, 1749 Thomas Lewis void, now Richard Harvey, 1759 Brace Webb, 1765 – Hicks, 1770 Mrs Seale, 1775 Edward Jones.

No. 59
1709 no entry, 1712 Mr Francis Brickley, 1713–1714 Mr Richard Ferryer, 1717 Mr Grant, 1718 to at least 1745 John Crosby, 1749 John Marks, 1754 Samuel Lowder, at no. 28 in 1775.

Nos. 61/3
first entry 1725 Elizabeth Hollister, 1754 Revd. Mr Gregory, 1775 Mrs Gregory, no. 29 in 1775.

No. 65
1727 Captain Barnes, 1745 John Mitchel, 1749 Stephen Pitt void, now Mr Stokes, 1754 Thomas Stokes void, 1759 Mr Andrews, 1775 William Hipsly, at no. 30 in 1775.

No. 67
1727 Captain Joseph Barnes, 1754 John Wade, 1759 Revd. Mr Raymond, 1775 Mary Bodman, at no. 31 in 1775.

No. 69
1721 Mrs Elizabeth Burgess, 1727 Capt Pitts, 1733 Mr Kyrle, 1740 Edythe Kyrle, 1745 Conrad Smith, 1749 Revd Mr Gregory, 1754 Capt. Baber, 1759 Mrs Baber, 1775 Mrs Ann Hobbs, at no. 32 in 1775.

No. 71
1721 Mr John Constant, 1736 widow Constant, 1745 Dr Burnett, 1749 James Stewart, 1754 Mrs Jones, 1759 Capt. Dolman, 1765 Samuel Newman, at no. 33 in 1775.

The two plots sold to William Matthews in August 1732
On the west side of Tinkers' Close a plot of void ground was sold by Thomas Holmes gent. to William Matthew merchant in August 1732, extending southwards from the highway leading to the Royal Fort to the west part of the tenement late of John Tilladam gent. (in Park Lane), eastwards to a summer house of John Thomas gent., thence to the back door of John Crosby (at nos. 61/3 St Michael's Hill), thence to the Fort Lane; the sale included two stables lately built by Holmes (behind no. 53 St Michael's Hill) (AC/JS 8(3)).

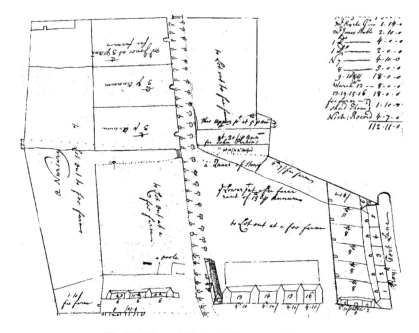

Fig 36. Plan of Tinkers' Close, c.1735–55

On the east side of Tinkers' Close a plot of void ground was sold by Thomas Holmes gent. to William Matthew merchant in March 1733, extending from the corner of John Elbridge's garden wall on the north to the corner of the house late of John Tilladam gent. on the south, thence to the corner of John Tyler's house, thence north to the corner of the garden of Thomas Wear gent. (AC/JS 8(8)). In 1736 part of this plot was sold to the Corporation, to prevent any houses being built upon the plot to the annoyance of the residents of the Royal Fort (00922; plan in 04479(1) fol.90).

The first parts of these two plots to be built upon were on the south side of Royal Fort Road and on the east side of Tankards Close, shown on a plan of before 1755 (see below, nos. 1–5 Royal Fort Road; the plan is undated but an annotation shows land sold to Harford in 1755; on an accompanying schedule information referring to 1738 onwards has been added).

Nos. 1–4, Royal Fort Road, south side (demolished)
These four houses were probably built by 1755, possibly by 1737. In 1791 these were the four adjoining tenements fronting Fort Lane, late of – Lewis, – Jenkins, Thomas Miles and Eleanor Arthur, by 1795 of Clarke, Jenkins, Ward and Stephens, conveyed by Thomas Sarjeant lime burner to Timothy Powell and his trustees (University Deeds 165).

No. 5 Royal Fort Road and no. 14 Tankards Close (demolished)

A house of the eighteenth century, of two storeys with the roof set back behind a parapet, is shown on a photograph of c.1930 (Winstone 1979 (102)). This house was probably built by 1755, possibly by 1737. By 1761 this was the tenement together with an adjacent house (see no. 14 Tankards Close) fronting Fort Lane. In 1816 it was the two tenements used as one built on part of Tankards Close by John Norman, after of William Pearce and since of Richard Ellison (University Deeds 94).

Nos. 1–7 Tankard's Close (demolished)

The west part of the land on which these houses were built was in 1735 the plot of void ground 20ft wide leased by William Matthew merchant to John Perkins cordwainer, from 1809 of Samuel Seyer, sold to John Thomas architect of Clifton and others for building in 1812. The middle part of the same land was in 1755 the plot of void ground 51ft 8ins wide towards the road leading through Tinkers' Close towards the Park, extending back on the north to land of Edward Harford merchant, sold by Jarrit Smith esq. to Harford. This became part of the gardens belonging to the house over and south of the Royal Fort gatehouse (04479(1) fols.201a and b).

These lands were sold by Richard Bedford and others to John Thomas architect of Clifton and others for building in 1812. The east part of the same was the plot of void ground 25ft 6ins wide to the road leading from the close to the Royal Fort, similarly sold for building in 1812. The building lease of 1812 included a specification, plan and sample elevation of the houses to be built (University Deeds 175). The occupants of nos. 1–5 had use both of the rain water cistern behind the houses and the use of the well originally made by William Matthew (University Deeds 123).

Nos. 8 and 9 Tankards Close (demolished)

These were the two tenements built by Thomas Sarjeant limeburner on land conveyed to him in 1787 (University Deeds 164 for 8 Tankards Close, plan shows the two houses with wash houses projecting forward on the street frontage).

Nos. 10 and 11 Tankards Close (demolished)

In 1740 no. 10, and possibly no. 11, were the tenement(s) conveyed by Nicholas Record house carpenter, William Tully meal merchant and John Dalton brickmaker to Henry Vaughan mariner. In 1791 no. 11 was the dwelling house now of Samuel Sadler as tenant to Samuel Seyer clerk, adjoining to a tenement formerly conveyed to Henry Vaughan mariner and now of Garland Andrews on the south and a piece of void land formerly of William Matthews merchant but now the garden of a tenement in Fort Lane of Thomas Taylor on the north, granted by Thomas Bonville and others with no. 10 to Seyer in 1790, and now granted by Seyer to Thomas Sarjeant ropemaker (University Deeds 174). By 1816 it was formerly of Samuel Daley now of – Walker (University Deeds 94).

No. 15 Tankards Close (demolished)
In 1816 this was the tenement lately built by Thomas Taylor decd. late in the occupation of Mary Morgan widow (University Deeds 94).

No. 17 Tankards Close (demolished)
In 1785 no. 17 was the new erected coach house with a stable, adjoining, conveyed to Thomas Sarjeant, by 1791 converted into two, of Richard Hart-Davis and – Pufer (University Deeds 165).

Nos. 19, 20, 21 and 22 Tankards Close (demolished)
In 1791 nos. 19–22 were four adjoining tenements to the rear of the tenement late of – Lewis, late of William Potter, William Barnes, Thomas Sarjeant and James Light, by 1795 of Potter, – Viner, – Jenkins and Light; from 1810 these were owned by William Lewton Clark (University Deeds 165).

Nos. 25 and 26 Tankards Close (demolished)
These two houses were built at the back of the garden of no. 69 St Michael's Hill, the plot first leased by Robert Holmes to Elizabeth Burgess in 1718; a deed of 1779 was possibly made in association with the construction of the two houses (University Deeds 32).

Nos. 34, 35 and 36 Tankards Close (demolished)
These three houses were evidently built by 1792, the date of the will of Samuel Loader, resident at no. 59 St Michael's Hill (University Deeds 119).

Nos. 37 and 38 Tankards Close (demolished)
No. 38 was Prior Cottage, in 1816 of John Rowe, High Park Avenue being formerly Crosby Lane (University Deeds 217). The locations of the two houses are shown on the City Valuer's plan (University Deeds 253). These houses were probably built by 1712, being those entered in the ratebooks between the entries for nos. 57 and 59 St Michael's Hill.

Occupancy from the ratebooks:

A. 1709 no entry, 1712–1714 Mr Thomas Summers, 1717 Summers now Mrs Huffolman, 1718 widow Sumers, 1719 probably Mr Perryman, 1722 James Tudor now Clack; 1733 Mr Saunders now Bolster, 1735 Dr Swaile, 1740 Jeremiah Swale void, 1745 David Crone, 1749 Capt. Punter, 1754 Madam Bray or Capt. Punter, 1759 Capt. Punter, 1770 Mrs Punter's, 1775 William Holbrook.

B. 1709 no entry, 1712–1719 Samuel Tedder, 1722 Capt. Thomas Stephens, 1733 now Sommers, 1736 Mr Pritchett, 1741 Richard Williams now Hale, 1745 Richard Bidmead, 1749 Thomas Lewis void, now Richard Harvey, 1759 Brace Webb, 1765 – Hicks, 1770 Mrs Seale, 1775 Edward Jones.

No. 39 Tankards Close (demolished)
Before 1811 this was part of the curtilage of no. 53 St Michael's Hill, conveyed to John Hale mariner in 1744, part of the estate of Sarah Hale spinster in 1795. In 1811 this was the 'Upper Garden' at the rear of no. 53 St Michael's Hill, then of Mary Till Adam; there is no mention of a house on the Upper Garden at this date (University Deeds 150).

Nos. 40 and 41 Tankards Close (demolished)
These houses were probably built by 1755, possibly by 1737 (see undated plan, AC/JS 8(61)). In 1791 these were the two tenements adjoining, late of Eleanor Hebb and Joseph Board, by 1795 of Frew and Sattle (University Deeds 165). By 1811 these were the premises of William Lewton Clark (abuttals from no. 39).

In 1811 no. 41, Hope Cottage, was the tenement late of John Southcott, purchased by William Lewton Clark from the executors of Anthony Palmer Collings esq. In the same year the property was conveyed by Clark to the Revd. Shute and others (University Deeds 141).

Nos. 42, 43 and 44 Tankard's Close (demolished)
These houses were probably built by 1755, possibly by 1737 (see undated plan, AC/JS 8(61)). In 1791 these were the three tenements in Tinkers' Close late of Mary Morgan, Joseph Read and – Newman, by 1795 of Morgan, Thompson and Newman, sold at auction to William Lewton Clark (University Deeds 165). In 1900 these were formerly of William Lewton Clark (University Deeds 65).

No. 45 (demolished)
In 1791 this was the stable late of – Edwards and adjoining to the back part of the tenement of Mary Morgan (see no. 42). In 1900 this was formerly of William Lewton Clark (University Deeds 65).

No. 46, Park Gate Cottage (demolished)
In 1791 this was probably the stable late of – Kirby and then converted into a tenement, adjoining to tenement late of Joseph Board, sold at auction to William Lewton Clark (University Deeds 165). The location of the house is shown on the City Valuer's plan (University Deeds 253).

No. 48, Park Gate House in 1896 (demolished)

The south elevation of a house of the eighteenth century, probably built by 1737 (see below), is shown on a photograph of the 1950s (20894). It was of one room in depth and three storeys, with the roof set back behind a parapet, a turret probably for the stairs projecting forwards on the south.

In 1737 the west part of the garden was that of William

Fig 37. Park Gate House, 1950s

Duckinfield, whose house and garden are noted here in the ratebooks for 1745. By 1785 it was the garden of Mr Russell with a summer house at the west end (University Deeds 108). In 1835 this was the tenement and garden of Charles Arthur Latcham, in 1868 formerly of John Weeks and then of Edward Jones; the ground behind to the south was in 1868 of Jacob Strickland and others, sold at auction in 1896 when it was known as Park Gate House (University Deeds 125).

South-west corner of Tankard's Close

In 1737 this was the plot of void ground used as a garden, in the possession of Thomas Jones esq. (see no. 9/10 Vine Row) and sold to him by William Matthews merchant. Plans of 1785 and 1815 show the location of the plot (University Deeds 108, with plans).

Nos. 53–56 (demolished)

These four houses were probably built by 1755, possibly by 1737 (see undated plan, AC/JS 8(61)).

Fig 38. Tankard's Close, looking north to the Distillhouse (on left)

Nos. 50-59, the 'distillhouse' (demolished)

In 1749 this was the property conveyed by Jarrit Smith esq. to John Nourse and others, described as the enclosed shed called 'a distillhouse', and a warehouse adjoining, 15ft 3ins wide to the lane coming from 'the Fortlane', 31ft 6ins wide in depth 'towards a walk intended for a twine walk' leading from the park to the close, 16ft 9ins wide at the back, together with a walled plot of ground on the west, late of Duckingfield 79ft towards the road from the park, 74ft 10ins towards another lane leading to 'Tinkards Close', in breadth towards the back part of the garden now of the trustees of Joseph Swayne decd. 40ft 8ins, together with a 'small edifice' on the garden, the premises bounded on the north by a stable of the trustees and by another tenement next to the distillhouse and warehouse, towards the south with the way leading from the park, with the lane leading straight to the fort lane on the east part and with the lane leading to another part of the ground formerly Tinkards Close on the west. The distillhouse is shown on a plan of the mid-eighteenth century (AC/JS 8(61)).

By 1799 this was the former distill house and warehouse adjoining, now two tenements and gardens, formerly in the occupation of John Sarjeant sawyer and John Butler mason and now of Edward Jones yeoman and Henry Jones shoemaker, still described as two tenements in 1830 (University Deeds 169).

The distill house, warehouse and two tenements can be identified on a plan of 1884 as nos. 50, 59, 57 and 58 respectively (University Deeds 169). On a photograph of the 1930s the distill house appears to be a dwelling house of the eighteenth century, with an eaves cornice (Winstone 1979 (106)).

7. ST MICHAEL'S HILL, THE WEST SIDE SOUTH OF ROYAL FORT ROAD

St Michael's church, churchyard and rectory or vicarage
Together with the rectory or vicarage, the church and churchyard can be seen in plan as occupying the most southerly part of the contiguous block of properties extending northwards to no. 51 St Michael's Hill. Investigating further the history of the church, churchyard and rectory or vicarage has not formed part of this study.

Nos. 23–51 St Michael's Hill
Nos. 23–51 St Michael's Hill share or shared a common rear or western boundary, indicating that the individual tenements are sub-divisions of what was formerly one plot. Since the earliest such sub-division so far recorded is of c.1483, for nos. 31–41 part of the endowment of Foster's Hospital, the subdivision of the plot as a whole is likely to have begun by that date (Manchee 1831, 1, 82).

Nos. 23–29 St Michael's Hill
This row of four houses was built in the seventeenth century, possibly c.1637 when nos. 27–29 were first recorded. The houses were apparently built as two pairs, were each built to be one room in depth, each of three storeys with attic gables to the street. On analogy with nos. 31–37, the four houses were probably built in a garden formerly occupied by a single summer house.

Fig 39. Nos. 23-9 St Michael's Hill, 1999

Nos. 27 and 29 were built by 1637, when they were demised by Humphrey Andrewes to his cousin Philip Bowcher the younger (BRO, Wills). In 1663 this was the tenement of Richard Cox (abuttals from nos. 31–41), assessed for two hearths in 1668 (F/Tax/A/1). In 1701 a lease of 'the Rose Alehouse' was granted by Edward Saunders of Axbridge to Solomon Edwards, sadler. Widow Tyly occupied his property in 1705. By 1736, when a new lease was granted by Edward Fuller the elder and Edward Fuller the younger to Gilbert Cobb, the house was in the tenure or occupation of Mary Whitmore, widow (deeds for no. 29 held by the owner of 'The Rose Again'; P/StM/land tax 1705).

Occupancy from the ratebooks:

No. 23

1695 Henry Berry, assessed for 6 windows, 1696, 1698–9, 1703–1705 Henry Berry, 1707 Mr Langford, 1712 Mr Chaddock for Penningtons, 1713–1722 Benjamin Chaddock, 1733 William Quinton, 1740 Henry Page, 1745 Capt. Thomas Collis, 1749 widow Collis, 1755 Jonathan Hobbs, 1775 Thomas Williams, no. 14 in 1775.

No. 25

1695 Henry Boucher, assessed for 6 windows, 1698–9 Elizabeth Edwards, 1703–1707 Mrs Davidge, 1712–14 William Read, 1717–1719 Capt. Whitson, 1722 William Whittson now Samuel Hort, 1733 Mrs Wilson as was, 1737 Mrs Dyke, 1740 James Marshall, 1745 Mary Bishop, 1759 John Derwent, 1765 widow Derwent, no. 15 in 1775.

No. 27

1695 widow Jones, assessed for 6 windows, 1696, 1698–9 Martha Jones, 1703–1712 Benjamin Chaddock, 1713–14 John Elsworthy, 1717–1719 Mrs Watts, 1722 Jane Watts, 1733 Mrs Phoebe Watts, 1765 Thomas Crocker, 1770 Mrs Whitlaw, 1775 John Stephens, no. 16 in 1775.

No. 29

1663 Richard Cox (abuttals from nos. 31–41), in 1668 assessed for two hearths, 1695 Nathaniel Milner, assessed for 6 windows, 1696, 1698–9 Nathaniel Milner, 1703–1707 widow Tylee, 1712–1714 widow Mary Baskerville, 1717–1719 Mrs Prigg, 1722 Frances Prigg now Joseph Barnes, 1733 widow Mary Whitmore, 1745 late William Thomas now void, 1749 John Way, 1770 Thomas Wyatt, no. 17 in 1775.

Nos. 31–41 St Michael's Hill

Nos. 31–41 were the 'four tenements, a cottage and a garden, lying upon St Michael's Hill', part of the endowment of the Hospital of the Three Kings of

Cologne in 1483, founded by John Foster (Manchee 1831, 1, 82; 04335(4) fol.128). In 1664 a new lease was granted to Thomas Moore, merchant, of 'four messuages & one cottage & four gardens thereunto adjoyning & belonging and a great garden lying on the south east part of the said cottage' with a covenant within four years to rebuild the cottages or tenements 'being intended to be pulled down' (04335(8) fol.17). This did not apparently happen until after 1695 and before 1703, when it was acknowledged that a great sum had been 'laid out in rebuilding'. By 1728 three tenements and gardens were leased to Francis Elbridge, in the possession of Mr Willoughby, John Mitchel and Gilbert Cobb (04335(8) fol.175; 04043(4) fol. 322). The two northernmost can be shown to be nos. 39 and 41. The southernmost was the house and garden now occupied by nos. 31–7.

Nos. 31–37 St Michael's Hill

In 1701 this was the house of Gilbert Cobb (abuttals from no. 29), by c.1790 the site of the Chicken Alehouse, and not apparently rebuilt c.1695–1703 (04479(2) fol.98c). A plan of c.1790 shows this property as a single large garden, with the Chicken Alehouse occupying the south-east corner, a house of one room on each floor (04479(2) fol.98c). The combined evidence of leases (above) and rates (below) indicates that in 1662 this was the garden house on St Michael's Hill occupied by Mrs Elizabeth Cugley (F/Tax/1/A). The plot was redeveloped c.1813 (Manchee 1831, 1, 546), ten houses and Park Place now occupying the site of the former garden (38041/BMC/12/PL2 fol.60).

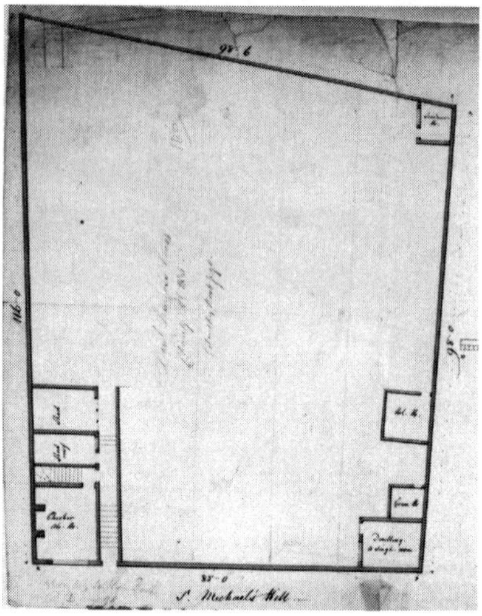

Fig 40. Nos. 31–7 St Michael's Hill, c.1813

Occupancy from the ratebooks:

1662 and 1668 Mrs Elizabeth Cugley's garden house, one hearth, 1673 possibly Thomas Standfast two hearths, 1695 (part of) Matthew Standfast four tenements, 1695 Thomas More, assessed for 12 windows, 1698–9 widow Standfast, 1703 Henry Berry for Mr Moor's garden and lodge, 1707–1718 Mr Henry Berry, 1719 and 1722 possibly Henry Berry, 1733 Gilbert Cobb, his garden in 1739, 1745 William Thomas, no. 18 the *Old Rose* in 1775.

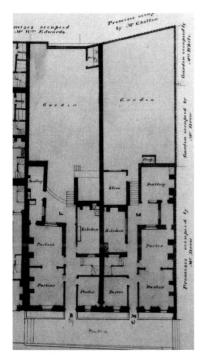

Fig 41. Nos. 39–41 St Michael's
Hill, 1861

Nos. 39 and 41 St Michael's Hill

These two houses were rebuilt between 1695 and 1703, each of three storeys with attic dormers, the ground floor in each probably arranged as two parlours and a kitchen cross-wing to the rear, each with a detached wash kitchen behind, shown on an outline plan of c.1800 and, for no. 41, on a more detailed plan of 1861 (04479(3) fol.63a; 38041/BMC/12/PL4 fol.37). The two houses were totally rebuilt in the 1950s, not even the stairs remaining; only the outside walls may be original.

Occupancy from the ratebooks:

No. 39

1696 Owen Williams (household listed), 1700 Henry Bird, 1703 Owen Williams in Mr Moors tenement, 1705 Sir John Duddlestone for Moore's new house, 1707–1722 Mr Benjamin Willoughby, 1733 Mrs Willoughby, 1755 Ann Dyer, 1759 Mrs Bristow, 1770 William Dymock, 1775 Mrs Bright, no. 19 in 1775.

No. 41

1696 probably Ezra Prigg (house-hold listed), 1698 probably John Hickes, 1700 Hannah Jones, 1705 madam Tucker, 1712–1713 Daniel Hickman, 1714 Daniel Hickman now widow Coysgarne, 1717–1719 Capt. Good, 1722 Joseph Percival, 1726 Mr David Deverell, 1733 Mr Deveral now Mitchel, 1740 John Mitchel, 1745 – Whadmore, 1749 Capt. Dolman, 1759 Mrs Dolman, 1765 Thomas Sims, no. 20 in 1775.

Nos. 43–7

In 1662 and 1668 this was Mr Hancock's garden house assessed for one hearth (F/Tax/A/1), in 1663 the tenement of Leonard Hancocke soapboiler (abuttals from nos. 39–41). By 1673 it was of Stephen Ruttland similarly assessed for one hearth, by 1679 the house and garden of the widow Rutland (F/Tax/A/4).

By 1689 there were two houses built, of the widow Moseley and Stephen Perkins. By 1697 these were the two tenements with gardens, between a garden now or late of Rowland Johnson on the south and a garden and certain housing of Eusebius Brookes merchant decd. on the north, extending back to a garden wall of William Lewis soapboiler (see Park Lane below), being the inheritance of Isaac Harper gent., on the west, lately purchased by Thomas Perkins merchant and Mary his wife decd. from Katherine Rutland of Henbury, and after the death of Thomas Perkins purchased from Mary his widow by John Knight, now sold by Knight and his wife Mary to Mary Roberts widow. In 1734 the two houses were purchased by John Cove goldsmith from Mrs Philpott the heiress of Mary Roberts, passing ultimately to Katherine Mitchell of Monmouth who sold both houses to Thomas King gardener in 1766, the occupants now Mrs Mannington and Mrs Cox (University Deeds 229).

King then rebuilt the two houses as three separate dwellings, nos. 43, 45 and 47, formerly nos. 11, 12 and 13 (University Deeds 264, 97 and 229). The three houses survive, and form a continuous row with no. 49 which must therefore have been rebuilt or at least refronted at the same time. Nos. 43 and 45 retain stairs and some interior trim of c.1770. In nos. 47 and 49 only a few features remain of the houses as rebuilt c.1770. The stairs and almost all the interior trim is of the 1950s or later.

Occupancy from the ratebooks:

Before 1689, see above, then divided:

No. 43
1689 widow Moseley, 1695 John Knight's tenement, 1695 widow Roberts 9 windows, 1703–1707 Isaac Crumpe [Mrs Roberts owner 1705], 1712–1713 Mrs Higgins widow, 1714 Mrs Higgins now Mr Moreton, 1715–1726 Mr John Moreton, 1733 Capt. Littlewood, 1740 Mr Torvell, 1755 Mrs Cove, 1765 Joseph Rossiter and occupier, 1770 John Thorn, no. 21 in 1775.

No. 45
1689 Thomas Perkins, 1695 Jonathan Allen 8 windows, 1695 Dr Collier, 1707–1717 Capt. James Gough, 1718 Mrs Gough, 1726 Mrs Phippen, 1732 Mrs Phippen now Stephens, 1733 Capt. Stevens, 1740 Capt. Derick Masters, 1745 Edward Bower, 1749 Richard Thomas now Thomas Wooten, 1755 Maria Mullington or Manaton, 1765 John Allen and Manaton, 1770 Maria Manaton, 1775 Martha Curtis, no. 22 in 1775.

No. 47
Built c.1770, 1770 Thomas Abbott, no. 22 in 1775.

Nos. 49–51 St Michael's Hill
No. 49 was rebuilt or refronted c.1770 when nos. 43–47 were built (see above). The interior of no. 49 has been totally rebuilt, only earlier outside

walls and possibly some partition walls remaining from before the 1950s. No. 51 does not form part of the row with nos. 43–49, but has also been almost entirely rebuilt internally.

Two houses were built here by 1679, occupied by Roger Buckstone and Alexander Newman, on land leased from Eusebius Brookes (F/Tax/A/4; Manchee 1831, 1, 133). In 1711 no. 49 was newly built by John Mereweather mason, no. 51 about to be rebuilt by Thomas Smith carpenter (see 09458(17)), the former evidently rebuilt or refronted c.1770 (see above).

Occupancy from the ratebooks:

No. 49
1679–1703 Alexander Newman, 1695 assessed for 6 windows, in 1701 the messuage and garden of Eusebius Brookes in the possession of Alexander Newman, 1705–9 Owens, 1712 late Daniel Tayler now Mr Pearson, 1713–1714 Mrs Pearson, 1717–1718 Richard Pey, 1722 probably John Lamprey now void, 1725 Mr Reves, 1726 widow or Mrs Smith, 1740 Revd. Humphrey Tucker, 1745 Mrs Tucker, 1749 Mrs Tucker now Mrs Cook, no. 23 in 1775.

No. 51
1679 Roger Buckstone, 1689 Joseph Saunders, 1695 John Millard, 1705–1709 Henry Bird, 1712–1718 Lady Whetstone, 1722 probably Mr

Fig 42. Nos. 39–57 St Michael's Hill from the rear, 1950s (University Library, Special Collections)

Jeremiah Deverell, 1726 Revd. Mr Tucker, 1740 Jacob Peloquin void, 1745 Mrs Parker, 1749 Mrs Good void, 1755 Mrs Webb, 1759 Mrs Gravatt, 1770 Capt. Henderson, 1775 Thomas Edwards, at no. 24 in 1775 (location confirmed in deeds for no. 49 and no. 51).

8. THE LITTLE PARK

By the late fourteenth or early fifteenth centuries a substantial and roughly rectangular block of land to the north of Park Row and a little to the west of St Michael's Hill formed part of the lands of the de Cheddar family. Through the marriage of Joan the daughter of Thomas Cheddar to Robert Talbot Viscount Lisle and illegitimate son of Edward IV, this land became part of the estate in Bristol of the Viscount Lisle who died in 1542, purchased by the Corporation from the Crown in 1544 (BRS 12, 27–8). The precise boundaries of this estate can be mapped from the information contained in deeds of the late eighteenth and early nineteenth centuries (Figs.9–12).

Within the Bristol Record office are three discrete sets of records relating to the management of this estate. First there are some 38 documents almost certainly derived from the muniments of the Earle family who held the estate from the eighteenth to the twentieth centuries (8016(1–38)). Secondly there are the records relating to the purchase by the corporation from the Crown, the subsequent lease 'in fee farm' and then the collection of 'fee farm' rents from the property, from 1544 to the twentieth century (01028(23)). Thirdly there are deeds relating to the subsequent purchase of parts of the property, for educational and other purposes (Avon Deeds A22026/1). The University's title deeds for the parts of the Lisle estate still in its ownership constitute a fourth set of records. These include documents which are the counterparts of those in the City's possession and several valuable abstracts of title which summarise the constituent parts of the estate in the eighteenth century, together with a schedule of the fee farm rents conveyed by the inheritors of the estate to the University in 1948 (University Deeds 251 and other references as below).

In the British Library the Harleian Charters also include deeds relating to the Cheddar lands. In 1402 Sir Thomas Brook and Joan his wife, together with her son Richard Cheddre, leased to Nicholas Excestre a close called 'Warresclos' at the top of St Michael's Hill, between the churchyard of

St Michael's Church and land lately of Richard Cobyndon, which close was formerly held by Stephen Reve as tenant to Sir Thomas Brook (BL Harl. Ch. 46.G.37).

In 1479 two closes of land next to St Michael's Church were leased by Edward Lord Lisle to Thomas Croft esq. at 37s 4d p.a; the deed was later annotated as for 'Hill Houses Ground'. In 1531 when leased by Lord Lisle to John Kenn and his wife, the property was described as 'all that garden ground ... betweene the garden which Griffith Jonys tailor now holdeth of the said John Ken on the west parte and the little voide ground ... the parsonage house of Seynt Mychell ... on the easte parte and extendethe itselfe from the kynges highweye forwards on the south parte unto the mayne wall that closeth yn the grounde of the said John Ken backwards on the northe parte.' (8016(1–6)). In 1557, now part of the city lands, a 'howse and a close in the bacsyde therof' were held by Master Payne.

The property was sold by the Corporation in 1596 to Thomas Aldworth, the fee farm rent set at 37s 4d p.a., the property described as:

All that Capitall Messuage or Mansion House and two gardens thereunto adjoyning viz. one of the sd Gardens is lying on the east side of the same house and the other on the west side neere adjoyning to the sd house And also two other gardens on the east part of the said messuage whereof one is now in the tenure or occpacen of William Ellis Alderman and the other garden is now in the tenure or occupation of Thomas Hopkins Merchant adjoyning to the Vicaridge House of St Michael aforesaid And also one other garden lying on the west pte of the said messuage now or late in the tenure or occupacen of John Barker merchant adjoyning to a garden late in the tenure or occupacen of William Sprint decd And also one close of pasture ground near adjoyning to the sd house and gardens conteyning by estimacen eight acres be itt more or less all which premises are situate and being in the prsh of St Michael aforesd within the suburbs of the said City of Bristoll and late were in the tenure or occupacen of Christopher Kenn Esq. deced and now in the occupation of William Sawyer clothier and are walled about with a stone wall between the churchyard and the said vicaridge house of St Michael aforesd on the east pte and certaine gardens late in the tenure or occupation of the said william Sprint on the west pte and a lane leading from Brandon Hill unto St Michaels Church aforesd on the south pte and certaine other grounds late in the tenure or occupacen of the sd William Sprint on the north pte (8016(8)).

In 1628, by then described as 'a greate Mansion house, gardeins, and fower acres and an halfe of ground', it was late in the tenure of Mrs Murcott in fee farm (BRS 24, 57 & 157). From c.1660 the estate was leased in increasingly smaller land parcels, described now (in alphabetical sequence) within the discrete streets of the development:

The Little Park
Lower Church Lane
Lower Park Hill
Medical Avenue
Old Park Hill
Park Lane
Stile Lane
Upper Church Lane
Vine Row

The Little Park

In 1670 this was 'the Little Park', extending from the outward bounds of the land held by Thomas Price to the outward bounds of the said park, leased by Isaac Harper gent. to John Henry carpenter, new leases granted in 1672 to William Dunning merchant, and in 1690 and 1701 to James Dunning merchant (8016(14,21,36)). The Little Park as defined from 1670 onwards must have been the area not yet subdivided for houses and gardens.

Lower Church Lane, north side, St Michael's Church Lane in 1775

Rupert House, formerly no. 10 St Michael's Church Lane (demolished)

A drawing and photographs show this house to have been of at least three parts. The central part was of the seventeenth century, having an east end stack with diagonally set chimneys, and a chimneypiece on the ground floor bearing the inscription '16 S R M 74'; the chimneypiece is now in the Red Lodge wigwam (Bristol City Library, extra illustrated Latimer's Annals, vol.1; Winstone 1972 (44–50); BRSMG Mb1007). An archaeological evaluation was undertaken on the site in 1992; the area excavated was minimal (Bristol Archaeology n.d.).

'S R M' were the initials of Stubbs, Richard and Mary. In 1660 this was the property leased by Isaac Harper gent. to Richard Stubbs merchant, by 1670 a garden and lodge late in the occupation of Charles Goatts vintner and now of Richard Stubbs, between the vicarage house and its yard on the east and a garden of Isaac Harper being late the land of Hugh Brown alderman deceased on the west. Stubbs was to build within two years a substantial building of two rooms on each floor, two storeys and a half high. The lease was subsequently assigned to John Napper and surrendered by him to Harper in 1682 (8016(17)). In 1761 the property was described as formerly of Richard Stubbs and after of John Napper and Jane his

Fig 43. Llan House and Rupert house, drawing of the early twentieth century

widow (University Deeds 251). In 1780 it was the house and garden late of William Matthew, after of Elizabeth Ware widow and now of the Reverend Michael Vrankeen (abuttals from no. 3). By 1781 it was held by Samuel Wilmott carpenter, under a lease granted in 1730, the 'tenement, garden ground, summer house and stable', in the occupation of the Reverend Michael Vrankeen, now conveyed to Isaac Bence (A22026/1).

Occupancy from the ratebooks:
1679 Mrs Gay for Mrs Stubbs, 1696 Jane Napper, household listed, 1718 Capt. Richard Cheshire, 1724 Capt. Matthew, 1738 Mrs Elizabeth Ware, 1750 Thomas Day, 1758 Mr Bagnell, 1760 Michael Vranken, at no. 10 St Michael's Church Lane in 1775).

Llan House, formerly no. 9 St Michael's Church Lane (demolished)
The main part of Llan House was of the eighteenth century, of three storeys with a centrally placed pedimented entrance to the garden side; to the west was a lower two-storey range (Bristol City Library, extra illustrated Latimer's Annals, vol.1). An archaeological evaluation in 1992 showed that the foundations of part of the taller building were of medieval date (Bristol Archeology n.d.).

In 1662 this was probably the garden house or lodge of Elizabeth the widow of Hugh Browne, assessed for two hearths (F/Tax/A/1(a)). In 1670 this was late the land of Hugh Brown alderman decd. (abuttals from Rupert House), in 1761 described as the tenement and garden formerly of Hugh Brown esq. and late of William Shelstone or his tenants (University Deeds 251). In 1780 it was the 'late new built ... tenement with the outhouses, buildings, gardens' late of Benjamin Bristow corn factor, after of Mary his widow, then of Mark Knaresborough linen draper, and now of Isaac Bence (at no. 9 St Michael's Church Lane in 1775), now conveyed to him by William Benson Earle (A22026/1). In 1784 this was the tenement and garden belonging to and in the occupation of Mr Isaac Bence cordwainer (abuttals from no. 4).

Occupancy from the ratebooks:

1662 see above, 1679 Hugh Brown for house and garden, 1696 Capt. Whetstone gent., 1708 Mrs Driver, 1711 Madam Rogers, 1712 Capt. Wood Rogers two tenements, 1715 John Cove, 1728 Mrs Elizabeth Cove, 1748 Mrs Mitchell void, 1750 Benjamin Bristow's new house, 1758 Mr Dymmock, 1762 void, 1764 Mark Knaresborough, 1768 Dean and Tucker, 1774 Isaac Bence, at no. 9 St Michael's Church Lane in 1775.

Nos. 4–7, in 1775 described as being in St Michael's Church Lane (demolished)

The history of this property can be traced from at least 1698 (see below).

In 1754 this was the property with a summer house conveyed by Harry Earle esq. to William Seede apothecary, opposite the capital messuage also leased to Seede (University Deeds 251). In 1776 this was late Mr Seed's garden, the summer house formerly part of the property (P/StM/land tax) now forming part of the property to the west, probably that 'small part' held by Seed under leases of 1754 and 1768 (A22026/1). The south end wall of the summer house is shown on a photograph of Lower Church Lane taken in 1967, the opening at the ground floor entirely appropriate for a stable as described in the deeds; it was within the area designated for a desk top study in 1998 (BaRAS 1998, Plate 1).

In 1780 this was the garden ground late of Joseph Males, since of William Seed apothecary and now of his widow (abuttals from no. 3). In 1784 this was the plot now of George Gibbs gent., bounded on the east part by a tenement and garden belonging to and in the occupation of Mr Isaac Bence cordwainer (at 9 St Michael's Church Lane in 1775) and on the west by a tenement late belonging to Mr William Seede decd., but now the property of Mr William Geatrell of Jamaica merchant and in the occupation of George Gibbs, conveyed by William Benson Earle to Mr Richard Hill plasterer and William Daniel mason (University Deeds 251, plan endorsed on deed).

Occupancy from the ratebooks:

1698 Isaac Crumpe for a garden, 1705 the same for Mr Blackwell's garden, 1708 Isaac Crumpe 'a garden & a lodge', 1712 Charles Horne's garden, 1718 Dr Lane's garden, 1734 Mr Duckinfield's garden, 1736 Joshua Mayes's garden, 1745 void, 1746 William Seed.

Nos. 1–3, formerly no. 4 St Michael's Church Lane, before 1748 held with nos. 1–3 Lower Park Hill opposite (demolished)

Before 1748 nos. 1–3 formed part of a property that extended across both sides of Lower Park Hill. The history of this property prior to 1746 is set out under Lower Park Hill, west side, nos. 1–3. A substantial part of this pre-1746 house certainly stood on the site of nos. 1–3 Lower Church Lane.

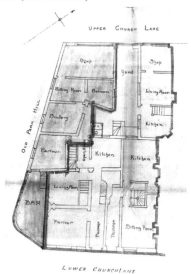

Fig 44. Nos. 1–3 Lower Church Lane, 1887

In 1776 this was the plot of void ground late allotted out and marked out for William Seede gent., 'on part whereof stood a large ruinous messuage' late of – Smith widow or her tenants, and on part whereof now stood 'a stable with a summer house over the same' now in the occupation of William Seede, who was to spend at least £200 on one or more substantial buildings to be constructed on the premises (A22026/1, plan endorsed on deed; note that the summer house was formerly part of the property to the east). In 1784 this was the tenement late belonging to Mr William Seede decd. (at no. 1 Back Church Lane in 1775) but now the property of Mr William Geatrell of Jamaica merchant and now in the occupation of George Gibbs (abuttals from no. 4).

In a desk top study prepared in 1998 it was concluded that the large ruinous messuage or house stood immediately to the west of Llan House and to the east of the summer house described in the previous entry. The further research undertaken for this study indicates that it is more likely to have been at the western end of Lower Church Lane, possibly like Rupert House and Llan House on the uphill part of the plot. A plan in the title deeds for no. 2 Upper Church Lane shows the buildings constructed on the western part of the plot by 1887, but gives no obvious clues to the location of the earlier house (17346).

Occupancy from the ratebooks of the part in Lower Church Lane, including the large ruinous house:

1746 Thomas Bidwell garden and tenement, 1762 – Derricour, 1764 Mrs Smith, at no. 4 in 1775, 1776 void ground.

See under Nos. 1–2 Lower Park Hill, south-west side, for the property before 1746.

South part of the Buildings Maintenance Department, formerly nos. 1 and 2 Lower Park Hill and the garden behind no. 1 (demolished)

Two buildings fronting Park Row, probably of the eighteenth century, are shown obliquely on a watercolour of the 1820s; these were built to the south of a larger house for which no illustrations survive (BRSMG M.2561).

Tracing the history of the property back through the ratebooks and assessments has shown that the large house which stood here was of a size comparable to that of the Red Lodge, and was in the earlier seventeenth century the dwelling of the owner of the Little Park estate.

At the entrance to the Little Park from Park Row this was the principal house on the estate, from at least the fourteenth century when it was part of the lands of the Cheddre family. It is clear from ratebooks and the deeds that the property extended across Lower Park Hill, the 'large ruinous messuage' occupying part of nos. 1–3 Lower Church Lane in 1754 being part of this same house.

On the south-west side of Lower Park Hill, this was in 1596 the capital messuage of Thomas Aldworth, by 1602 of Hugh Murcot vintner, by 1628 late of Mrs Murcott, then successively of Ralph Farmer, Isaac Harper and Thomas Prigg, who occupied the house in 1662. In 1665 the garden plot to the east of that leased to William Ballard was described as being 'behind the capital messuage then of Isaac Harper' (see Stratton's house and garden, to the north of the Park Row Asylum in Park Row). In 1690 Powell's garden house in Well Close (see Upper Church Lane) was described as being by the way coming up from the house of Isaac Harper, where Ralph Farmer late dwelt, and after Thomas Prigg dwelt. In 1710 a property slightly uphill from Park Row on the opposite side of Lower Park Hill was leased with free access through both the pavement and street door of the capital messuage of Isaac Harper formerly of Ralph Farmer clerk (see nos. 16–18 and the plot to the north east in Lower Park Hill). In 1761 this was the capital tenement, garden, outhouses, stables etc. theretofore of James Hasell decd. and after of Dr Lane (University Deeds 251, probably reciting an earlier description).

In 1776 the property belonged to William Benson Earle and was occupied by – Bevin spinster (abuttals from garden to west). In 1779 the greater part of the property comprised a tenement late of – Hastell coachpainter but now void, and a small tenement adjoining, occupied by Lewis Thomas shipjoiner, then conveyed by William Benson Earle to Richard Hill, subject to a yearly fee farm rent of 2s 6d (University Deeds 251, the location shown on an endorsed plan). Also conveyed by Earle to Hill was the garden ground behind no. 1, since at least 1776 of Thomas Andrews and others, together with a small summer house or edifice thereon

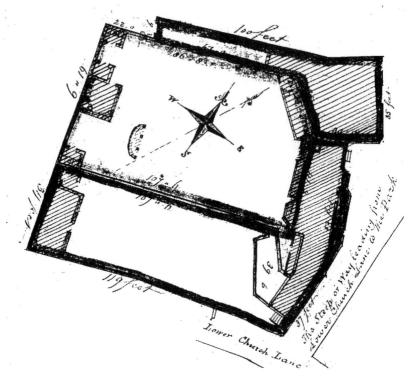

Fig 45. Nos. 1–3 Lower Park Hill, 1779

erected and built (University Deeds 251, the location shown on an endorsed plan; abuttals from garden behind nos. 2–3, see below).

Occupancy from the ratebooks:

pre-1748
1662 Thomas Prigg 7 hearths, 1664 10 hearths, 1679 possibly Joseph Knight, 1689 Sir John Knight (here or nearby) assessed for 7 hearths, 1695 Sir John Knight assessed for 20 windows (same as Red Lodge), 1698 Sir John Knight in James Hassell's house and garden, 1700 James Hassell esq., 1713 Dr Lane, 1715 Thomas Tiley esq., 1718 Mr Tyler (the same ?), 1727 Mr Hassell's house void, 1730 Mr Hassell's tenements, 1732 Simpkin's tenements, 1737 Mrs Sarah King's tenements, 1746 Thomas Bidwell for garden and tenements – for 1748 onwards:

Garden
(behind nos. 1 and 2) 1748 Mr Smith's garden, 1754 Pendry's garden, 1756 John Probert's garden, 1762 late Marchant's garden, 1766 Revd. Seyer's garden, 1776 Richard Hill's garden.

No. 1

1760 Marchant, 1762 Samuel Cook, 1772 Betty Roberts, 1774 Hester Carpenter, 1776 Martha Sheppard.

No. 2

1762 Stephen Stringer, 1766 Josiah Ashley, 1770 Mary Bartlett, 1772 Mary King, 1774 Betty Bevins (at nos. 1–2 in 1776 – University Deeds 251).

and see also under nos. 1–3 Lower Church Lane.

Middle part of the Buildings Maintenance Department, formerly the garden behind nos. 2–3 (demolished)

In 1776 this was the garden ground 'in the Park' conveyed by William Benson Earle esq. to Richard Hill, by 1779 occupied by Isaac Bence. In 1814 this formed part of the property conveyed by Hill's executors and James Ireland Wright to William Richard Todd; the plan endorsed on the deed shows in detail the various buildings constructed in the garden. Together with various additions to the houses on the Lower Park Hill frontage (University Deeds 251 including abuttals from nos. 1–2).

Towards the north part of the Buildings Maintenance Department fronting Lower Park Hill, formerly no. 3, also until 1809 the garden behind and to the north (demolished)

By 1748 this was possibly John Brickdale's stable (see ratebooks, below). From 1754 it was held by William Seed, owner of the property on the opposite side of Lower Park Hill (see under Upper Church Lane).

By 1776 the garden ground behind was in the possession of Thomas Stratton linen merchant (abuttals from nos. 1–2 Lower Park Hill). In 1784 William Benson Earle sold to Richard Hill, plasterer and tiler, and William Daniel, mason, the garden ground, stable, workshop and other buildings, behind nos. 1–3. These were now occupied by Thomas Stratton, linen merchant, and William Morgan, carpenter. In 1809 the north part of the property, excluding no. 3, was sold separately (see below).

In 1814 nos. 1–3 and the gardens immediately behind were conveyed in their entirety by the trustees of Richard Hill, deceased, to Mr James Ireland Wright and to Mr William Richard Todd, a detailed plan showing plans of the buildings and the various parts of the property as purchased at different dates (University Deeds 251). The house is shown on the 1828 map.

Occupancy from the ratebooks:

1748 John Brickdale's stable, 1756 William Seed's coach house and stable, 1766 Robert Simpson's workshop, 1776 William Morgan's workshop.

(behind and uphill of no. 3) 1748 John Brickdale's garden, 1755 Thomas Stretton's garden and stable, 1766 William Seed's garden.

The north part of the Buildings Maintenance Department fronting Lower Park Hill, formerly nos. 4 and 5 (demolished)

In 1809 this was the part of the above property sold by Richard Hill to Matthew Brickdale, the outline of the garden and the houses at the east end of the plot shown on the plan endorsed upon the deed, described as a plot of garden ground with a stable and coach house formerly workshops and other build-ings now of Richard Hill and Richard Brickdale. In 1818 the property was sold by Matthew Brickdale to Danvers Ward, the stable and coach house shown on a plan endorsed on the deed (University Deeds 251). These had been demolished by 1828, being replaced by the two rows of four and two houses respectively, shown on the 1828 map and on a plan within a conveyance of 1907 (University Deeds 251).

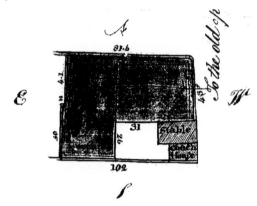

Fig 46. Corner of Lower Park Hill and Medical Avenue, 1818

Medical Avenue

Stretton's house and garden, to the north of the Park Row Asylum
On the north side of the Buildings Maintenance Department car park is the surviving part of a garden and house wall, part built in stone, part in brick. This can be identified as part of a property existing by the 1660s. No illustrations of the house prior to its demolition or destruction have been traced.

In 1665 this was the garden seven by five perches (i.e. 115ft 6ins by 82ft 6ins) leased by Mr Harper to William Ballard bookseller, part of one close formerly two, behind the capital messuage then of Isaac Harper and lying at the south end of the same close, between a garden of John Gonning esq. on the south (see no. 17 Park Row), a little lane leading from Stony Hill up to a garden called 'Collonell Birches' then of alderman Jackson on the west, a piece of ground then intended to be made into a garden by John Bevill on the north, the said close or closes on the east, together with a way leading to the granted ground 'in, by and through' the gate of the said capital messuage along the north side of the garden wall, together with use of the well in Harper's close. Subsequently of Henry Jones (the 1761 description in University Deeds 251 reciting a much earlier deed), from 1691 this was leased by Isaac Harper gent. to William Stretton mariner, with 'the dwelling house and garden thereon erected and standing', in 1732 leased by alderman Robert Earle and brother of Joseph Earle deceased to Anne Stretton the widow of Joseph Stretton mariner.

In 1786 this was the plot described as 'Mr Thomas Stretton's house and garden', sold by William Benson Earle esq. to Mr Richard Hill, now a garden ground with a dwelling, greenhouse, laundry and scullery since erected, partly on the north-east side of ground of, and partly on land adjoining, the freehold inheritance of Thomas Stretton, bounded on the south-east by other lands of Stretton (east of the Park Row Asylum) and also by lands of Dr Cobb (the Park Row Asylum), on the south-west by lands of Ann Brain spinster (later the synagogue site) (University Deeds 243, bundle 2). In 1807 this was sold by Mr Richard Hill to Mr Robert Meaby, on the south-east the lands formerly of Cobb then of – Lucas and now of Thomas Edwards linen draper, on the south-west the lands formerly of Ann Brain spinster now of Matthew Wright merchant (the synagogue site). The dwelling, greenhouse, laundry and scullery mentioned in the 1786 deed are shown only schematically on the 1807 plan, the short length of return wall with two openings to the east corresponding exactly to the structure shown here on the 1828 map. In 1809 it comprised the premises and garden belonging to Mr Robert Meaby, formerly of Thomas Stratton. By 1831 the property was held by the Revd John Leifchild, sold then to Mr John E Lewis, by 1857 of John Stewart Lewis (University Deeds 243 including abuttals from adjacent properties).

For the property to the east see Lower Park Hill

Old Park Hill, north-east side

At the corner with Upper Church Lane (demolished)
In 1754 this was the messuage and small tenement of John Cheston baker (abuttals from nos. 1–4 Upper Church Lane). In 1780 this was part of the property late of William Seede, now conveyed by William Benson Earle to Mary Seede (A22026/1, annotated 'Q Coulson', with plan endorsed).

Occupancy from the ratebooks:

1748 Mary Jones, 1752 – Foord, 1754 Cheston, 1756 Mr Seed snr., 1762 Thomas Seed, 1764 widow Seed, 1766 – Lewis, 1768 Thomas Crocker.

No. 12 (or very close) and to the south, the Well House, now within the site of St Michael's School
In the early eighteenth century this was the little tenement called the 'Well

House', at or over the public well, in or near the close called the Park or Well Close, late of James Hasell or his tenants (University Deeds 251). In 1780 this was the tenement 'commonly called the wellhouse' now of Richard Hazard Porter', one of three properties which were said to 'join together', the boundaries of the plot and the location of adjacent properties shown on the plan endorsed on the deed (A22026/1).

For the plot to the south see Upper Church Lane.

Occupancy from the ratebooks:

1679 widow Taylor [Tyley ?] for [park, ground and] well house, 1698 – Fisher for the well house, 1698 Mr Gough for the well house, 1703 John Beale 'in the well house', 1705 'John Beale for Fisher's house over the well', 1706 John Beale, 1707 John Owen, 1710 Elizabeth Fisher, 1744 Mrs Edwards, 1752 widow Miles or Mills, 1766 Richard Price, 1768 Elizabeth Roberts, 1770 Mr Jones, 1774 Ann Morgan, 1776 William Jenkins, 1778 Richard Hazard.

No. 14 and the plot to the north-east, in part the site of St Michael's School (demolished)

In 1660 this was the property leased by Isaac Harper gent. to Edward Tiley brewer, the ground late enclosed at the lower end of the great ground, 'lying near the pool there', together with the dwelling house, wash house and buildings erected by Tiley, and with a small ground lying between the well house and a wall then built by Jonathan Blackwell. The dwelling house can be identified as the 'garden house' held by Edward Tyly and assessed for 5 hearths in 1662 and 1668 (F/Tax/A/1(a) St Michael's parish). In 1690 the property was leased by Isaac Harper to Ann Berrow widow, one of Tiley's daughters, in 1693 to Frances Lane widow (8016(27)).

In 1780 this was 'the tenement, garden, stable and premises' now of Hannah Camplin widow, also 'a tenement with the garden' now of John Brown, also the wellhouse (see above). These were said to 'join together', the boundaries of the plot and the location of adjacent properties shown on the plan endorsed on the deed (A22026/1).

Occupancy from the ratebooks:

1689 widow Tylyes house, 1691 Ann Tylle, 1695 James Matucks, 1696 household listed, 1698 Samuel Pain, Peter Davis, 1703 ? William Horne, 1705 Isaac Taylor, 1708 Capt. Robert Edwards for Mr Gray, 1718 Mr Wall ?, 1723 George Blake, 1725 Joseph Patch, 1727 Capt. Richard Lewis, 1750 Mrs Lewis, 1752 John Davis, 1754 William Davis, 1756 Jeremiah Swayle, 1764 John Saice, 1770 John Brown, 1782 William Pritchard.

Nos. 16–18, 3–4 Old Park, and the plot to the north-east

Two houses of the seventeenth century were much altered in the 1920s and restored in the 1980s.

These houses are built upon the plot described before c.1710 as the 'parcel of ground formerly marked and measured out to be enclosed by one Thomas Deane, ... at the lower end of a Great Ground ... adjoining to the garden formerly of Edward Tyly there and containing in length eight perche[s] and in breadth four perch[es] ... all houses, erections and buildings thereon now ... late ... of Nicholas Hicks' or his tenants (conveyance of 1 and 2nd October 1761 reciting a much earlier description, University Deeds 251). The measurements in perches give a length of 132ft and breadth of 66ft, corresponding almost exactly to the dimensions of this plot as later mapped. In 1710 this was the parcel of ground heretofore marked out to be enclosed by Thomas Deane, now deceased, lying at the lower end of Isaac Harper's ground adjacent to a garden heretofore of Edward Tyley, eight perches long and four perches wide, with free access through both the pavement and street door of the capital messuage of Isaac Harper formerly of Ralph Farmer clerk (i.e. up Lower Park Hill) and by the alley next to the churchyard of St Michael's (i.e. Park Lane or Back Church Lane), also with free access to the well near to the demised premises, the property now granted by Isaac Harper to James Maddox gent (8016(31)). By the early 1740s the property comprised the dwelling houses of James Madocks and of the widow Webb, together with a summer house and garden ground in the possession of William Scamell; on the north was the Little Park, on the west the way leading to the park, on the south the tenement of Mr Richard Lewis mariner and the garden of Mr Burgess, on the east a way leading from Church Lane to another part of the Park (loose paper with 8016(31), an undated assignment, dated by the Land Tax entries to the early 1740s).

Fig 47. Nos. 3–4 Old Park from the rear, 1920s

Occupancy from the ratebooks:

No. 16

1698 widow Dean for two tenements (this and that below), 1705 widow Dean for house and garden, 1710 widow Dean void, 1712 Peirce Bally, 1723 James Henly, 1728 James Headly now Griffiths, 1730 Mr Scrill, 1732 Elizabeth Webb, 1746 Mrs Pope, 1748 Mrs Tisehurst, 1750 Capt Saunders,

1756 – Cheston, 1758 Walter Perkins, 1766 Robert Combe, 1768 – Newell, 1770 William Crosse, 1772 Mr Redripp, 1776 Richard Millett.

No. 18
1662 Thomas Deane, assessed for 4 hearths, 1668 assessed for 1 furnace, 1 oven, 4 hearths, 1679 widow Dean house and garden, 1698 widow Dean for two tenements (this and the above), 1705 Robert Hawkesworth for widow Dean's house and garden, 1709 Mrs Baskerville, 1711 William French, 1716 James Maddox, 1746 Revd Barjew, 1748 – Stokes, 1750 Richard Rogers, 1764 Jabez Marchant, 1766 Richard Walkely, 1774 Mrs Walkely, 1775 James Mason, at no. 33 Park in 1775, 1776 Samuel Clark, 1780 Martha Langdon, 1782 George Watkins.

The garden on the south side of Old Park, generally rented with the above
Sometimes but not always rented with the above was the garden to the north-east; the 1828 map shows summer houses in the upper corners.

Occupancy from the ratebooks:

1705 widow Millerd for widow Dean's garden, 1706 Mrs Dean's garden, 1710 William French for Mrs Dean's garden (after which it is suggested that it is part of his and then James Maddox's tenure of the adjacent house); next entry is 1727 widow Bartlett's garden, 1730 Mr Rogers' garden, 1731 Dr Barrett's garden, 1736 William Scammell's summer house and garden, 1752 Richard Rogers, 1764 Jabez Marchant for summer house and garden, 1766 Richard Walkely, 1774 Mrs Walkely, 1776 Mr Haskins for garden.

Old Park Hill, south-west side

The south-west side of Old Park Hill was developed as a row of ten houses from 1714 onwards. Photographs and plans show that the houses were of three storeys with attics, two rooms in depth with detached kitchens to the rear, some with shell hoods to the doorcases (see Winstone 1981 (60)). All are now demolished.

Amongst the first building leases granted by the owner Joseph Earle esq. were those of 1714 to Mr John Brickdale woollen draper at no. 11, to Nathaniel Beale tiler at no. 13 and to Joseph End house

Fig 48. Old Park Hill, street frontage

Fig 49. Old Park Hill, detached
kitchen to rear

carpenter at no. 17. The leases each stipulated that there be built one substantial messuage, three storeys high and costing at least £100. By 1719 nos.
15 and 17 had been built, the former by John Price house carpenter. No. 29,
built by James Lewis house carpenter, had been completed by 1722. The row
was completed and occupied by 1723 (A22026/1; University Deeds 251).

Occupancy from the ratebooks:

No. 11
1723 John Brickdale esq., 1768 void, 1770 William Hillhouse, 1772 James
Cockburn, 1774 Capt. Thomas Fitzherbert, no. 4 Park in 1775.

No. 13
1723 Capt. Atwood, 1727 Mrs Kanah, 1728 Capt. Smith, 1736 widow
Smith, 1738 Capt. Edward Tovey, 1748 Capt. Smith, 1760 widow Smith,
no. 5 Park in 1775.

No. 15
1718 John Price, 1725 Capt. Skinner, 1727 Capt. William Barry, 1732
Jacob Peloquin, 1736 Mrs Shanks, 1740 George Griffin, 1748 Benjamin
Boulton, 1750 Mrs Griffin, 1758 Mrs Denny, 1764 Lawrence Ormerod,
1768 Mrs Alicia Rich.

No. 17
1718 Capt. Phippes or Phelps, 1727 Mrs Tudor, 1732 Capt.
Mackenzie,1735 Madam Walter, 1738 Capt. Griffin, 1742 Mary Shuter,
1746 Mrs Griffin, 1752 Mrs Gough, 1770 Charles Horwood, 1774 George
Luther, no. 7 Park in 1775.

No. 19

1723 Benjamin Hancock, 1725 William Jordan, 1736 West, 1738 Capt. John Ross, 1744 Capt. Franks, 1754 Joseph Kelson, no. 8 Park in 1775.

No. 21

1723 widow Stratton, 1725 Revd. Robert Clark, 1728 Mr Deane, 1732 Mrs Haynes, 1734 Thomas Jones, 1738 Mr Worgan, 1739 Mr Harris, 1740 Joseph Jefferies, 1748 Capt. Tovey, 1750 Mrs Tovey, 1764 Rev. Dursden, 1772 Mrs Cave, no. 9 Park in 1775.

No. 23

1723 John Hale, 1725 Capt. Sweet, 1728 Mr Hall, 1732 Christopher Jones, 1738 Capt. Henry Parker, 1748 widow Parker, 1750 Revd. Berjew, 1754 Mr Milner, 1756 John Webb, 1762 John Vaughan, 1768 Mrs Ann Vaughan, no. 10 Park in 1775.

No. 25

1723 Capt. Pope, 1725 Capt. Stratton, 1727 Mr Abel Dean, 1728 Revd. Mr Clark, 1732 Mr Hillhouse, 1734 Madam Haynes, 1739 Thomas Knee, 1740 Ralph Cox, 1744 widow Cox, 1748 John Foord, 1756 Mrs Harris void, 1758 Elizabeth Adey, 1762 Stephen Jenkins, 1768 Mrs Jenkins, 1770 Mrs Wraxall, , no. 11 Park in 1775 (no. 25 on conveyance of 1947, University Deeds 122, 1947).

No. 27

1723 Capt. Sweet, 1725 John Hall, 1728 Mrs Mary Day, 1746 Mrs Goodwin, 1756 void, 1758 John Scott, 1762 Elizabeth Blackmore, 1770 Mrs Jordan, 1772 Mrs Ann Evans, no. 12 Park in 1775 (no. 27 on conveyance of 1947, University Deeds 122, 1947).

No. 29

1723 Capt. Mullington, 1725 John Brite, 1725 Madam Bright, 1728 Mr Farmer, 1738 Mr Lewis, 1744 Mary Yemans, 1746 Thomas Willoughby, 1776 Mrs Willoughby, no. 13 Park in 1775.

Park Lane, east side

South of the Manor House, no. 2 Back Church Lane in 1775 (demolished)

In 1660 this was the part of the great ground 'walled in' by Charles Powell apothecary, and now leased to him by Isaac Harper gent. (8016(23)). By 1662 Powell had built a garden house, assessed for three hearths; by 1668 this was held by Thomas Williams, similarly assessed then, but only for two hearths in 1673 (F/Tax/A/1). Early maps and illustrations provide little information as to the appearance and precise location of the house.

From 1673 the property was leased by Harper to Thomas Williams merchant and Elizabeth his wife, executors of Powell's will, from 1690 leased by Harper to Robert Perry, bounded by the way (i.e. Upper Church Lane) to the south, leading from St Michael's churchyard to the dwelling house of Jonathan Blackwell (see Upper Church Lane) in or near which there had been a pool and by a garden then of Edward Hurne vintner and then late of Abraham Wild ropemaker (i.e. the Manor House) to the north; and by a way (i.e. Park Lane to the west) leading out of the way aforesaid to the garden late of Abraham Wild then of Edward Hurne and the churchyard and the garden (both on the east side of the plot) late of Gilbert Moore (8016(23)). Included in the lease to Robert Perry of 1690 was the way leading to the garden, 'as well as by and through the way opening into St Michael's churchyard as by the way coming up from the house of Isaac Harper, where Ralph Farmer and then Thomas Prigg both lived' (see nos. 1 and 2 Lower Park Hill); this last way must be Upper Church Lane (8016(23)).

In 1781 this was the tenement, garden, warehouse and premises now of John Bond custom house officer, sold by William Benson Earle to Richard Hill, tiler and plasterer, shown on a plan endorsed on the deed (A22026/1).

Occupancy from the ratebooks:

occupiers – 1662 Charles Powell (assessed for 3 hearths), 1689 Mr Mors (entries to here located from property holdings), 1695 John Tinall (assessed for 9 windows), 1696 Mr Tindall French minister, 1698 'Mr Champnys late tinneles voyd', 1698 Richard Champneys for a house and 2 gardens, 1705 Richard Champny's house burnt, 1709 Chamneys house burned, rebuilt but void, 1710 Daniel Commerline or Cumberland, 1744 Ann Cumberland, 1754 John Pardo, 1756 void, 1758 George Spearman, 1764 William Thomas, at no. 3 Back Church Lane in 1775.

To the east of the Manor House in Park Lane, on the north side of St Michael's churchyard, no. 3 Back Church Lane in 1775 (demolished)

A watercolour, drawing and photographs of before the Second World War show a house of the seventeenth century, built largely in stone, of two storeys and an attic, not jettied, its gable end

Fig 50. Park Lane / St Michael's churchyard, Gilbert Moore's house, drawing of late nineteenth century

facing the churchyard of St Michael's. In plan the house was of one or possibly two rooms in depth. Tall sash windows on the ground and first floors could be interpreted as alterations of the eighteenth century (Bristol City Library Loxton drawings 1707X; BRSMG M4023; Aerofilms 47090).

This house can be identified as the garden house of Gilbert Moore, assessed for two hearths in 1662; Moore's main residence was in Broad Street, in St Werburgh's parish (F/Tax/A/1). In 1691 this was the tenement formerly of Gilbert Moore barber surgeon now or late of Henry Totterdell mariner (abuttals from Manor House). In 1761, reciting much earlier deeds, this was described as the tenement and garden theretofore of Henry Totterdale then late of Henry Berry gardener (University Deeds 251).

Occupancy from the ratebooks:

1662 Gilbert Moore, 1695 [illeg.]win assessed for 9 windows, 1696 John Owen, household listed, 1719 Mr Berry's house in the churchyard, 1722 possibly John Heard, 1733 Henry Berry.

The Manor House, no. 31 Park in 1775

The Manor House is of the late seventeenth century, with earlier parts on the east and west. The main part of the house can be identified as the rebuilding of c.1691.

In 1662 this was possibly the 'garden house' held by Henry Jones, the entry in the hearth tax return being between the entries for the

Fig 51. The Manor House, Park Lane, 1950s

properties to the north and east, of Jordan and Moore. By 1668 the house had been rebuilt or much extended, now held by Edward Hurne vintner and assessed then and in 1673 for 11 hearths (F/Tax/A/1). Millerd's map shows the house iconographically, using the form adopted also for the Red Lodge and Royal Fort House.

In 1691 it was described as late of Abraham Wild ropemaker then of Edward Hurne vintner (abuttals from Powell's garden house in Well Close). In 1691 this was the tenement now demolished by fire, bounded on one side by the tenement or garden late of Charles Powell apothecary (to the south, see below) now or late of Thomas Morse or his tenants, and with an orchard formerly of Richard Jordan painter and now or late of John Moone sadler on the other (which must be the north side); and with a tenement formerly of Gilbert Moore barber surgeon now or late of Henry Totterdell mariner on one side (on the east) and the park or hill ground on the other (which must be on the west). Late of George Mason tobacconist as tenant to John Martin, the assignee of Edward Hurne vintner deceased, it was now leased by Isaac the heir of Isaac Harper to Joseph Earle merchant, Earle to spend at least £280 on rebuilding and providing a new substantial messuage within three years (8016(24)).

It is not known from what date the property was known as 'the Manor House'. The name is entirely appropriate, since it was from the 1690s the house of the owner of the estate, formerly the role of the house formerly of Isaac Harper, later of Sir John Knight, at the foot of Lower Park Hill (see nos. 1 and 2 Lower Park Hill).

Occupancy from the ratebooks:

1668 and 1673 Mr Hurne 11 hearths, 1679 Edward Hurne house and garden, 1696 Joseph Errell 20 windows, 1696 Joseph Earle, household listed, 1700 Capt. Joseph Earle, 1706 Joseph Earle esq., 1723 Joseph Earle and Mr Green, 1727 Col. Earle and Mrs Green, 1732 Alderman Earle, 1736 Henry Earle esq., 1742 William Ramsey, 1748 void, 1750 James Rosco, 1760 Mrs Rosco, 1772 William Williams.

No. 8, north of the Manor House (demolished)

North of the Manor House the property formerly of Richard Jordan (see below) was evidently divided by John Moone c.1698 (see below). Photographs of the 1950s show a gabled house at the north-west corner of this plot, only a part of the roof visible (20894). The doorcase with closed pediment on the elevation to Park Lane was of the early eighteenth century (Winstone, Bristol 1950-1953 (71)).

Occupancy from the ratebooks:

1698 William Turgis in John Moon's house, 1703 widow Yeamans, 1705 widow Yeamans for John Moone's house, 1706 Madam Yeamans, 1716 Joice Yeamans, 1723 Mr Yeamans, 1740 William Hopkins, 1746 John Lewis, 1752 Capt. Reed, 1754 John Rowland, 1756 George Sturmy, 1758 Theodocia Cobon, 1770 George Sturmy.

Richard Jordan's house (demolished)

Millerd's map of 1673 depicts a tall gabled house at the north-west corner of this property. This house may have been encapsulated within the house shown at this location on the Ordnance Survey map of 1884 and on photographs of the 1950s, prior to its demolition (including 20894). This house can be identified as the garden house held by Richard Jordan in 1662, assessed for three hearths, held by Jordan until his death in 1672; the rooms and contents are described in the inventory of his possessions (F/Tax/A/1; Bristol wills and inventories).

Fig 52. Richard Jordan's house, Millerd 1673

By 1691 this was the orchard formerly of Richard Jordan painter and now or late of John Moone sadler (abuttals from Manor House). By 1732 and 1733 it was late of John Till Adam gent., the location of the house accurately fixed by the deeds of sale for two parts of Tinkers' Close (see above). In 1761, reciting a much earlier survey, this was described as a tenement with wash kitchen, garden and orchard in or near the Park, theretofore of John Till Adam gent. and a tenement and garden built on part of the last mentioned by John Moone decd., all formerly of Susannah Moore or her tenants (University Deeds 251).

In 1766 this was the property of – Tuckey gardener (abuttals from no. 47 St Michael's Hill). In 1776 this was the tenement and garden now of Thomas Tisdale gardener, bounded on the north by the garden of Thomas Hill plumber, on the south by the garden of William Williams, on the east by the garden of Thomas Sims, and on the west by the way called the Park, sold by William Benson Earle to Thomas Sims merchant (A22026/1).

Occupancy from the ratebooks:

1662 Richard Jordan 3 hearths, 1668 – hearths, 1673 2 hearths, 1676 Richard Jordan painter (will and inventory), 1676 Richard Jordan painter (will and inventory), 1679 Philip Jordan house and garden, 1689 widow Jordan, in 1691 the orchard formerly of Richard Jordan painter and now or late of John Moone sadler, 1695 sheriff Lewis, assessed for 9 windows, 1697 William Lewis soapboiler (from abuttals for 43–7 St Michael's Hill) 1698 William Lewis in John Moone's house, 1705 John Tilladam for the same, 1725 Mr Giles, 1728 Mr Giles that was, 1730 William Bradford, 1738 Thomas King, 1742 John Hagley, 1756 Martin Pearce, 1760 William Tuckey, 1768 – Tesdal, 1772 William Barker, 1774 Mr May, 1776 William Basterfield.

Park Lane, west side

Later Pear Tree Cottage, immediately below Vine Row within the remnant of the Little Park, no. 28 Park in 1775 (demolished)

Pear Tree Cottage (named as such in the deeds, University Deeds 135) is shown most clearly on photograph of the 1950s and one of 1960; it was of three storeys and an attic, of one room on each floor, with a single-storey extension. The pitch of the gabled roof and the uniformity of the fenestration indicated that it was of the eighteenth rather than the seventeenth centuries (20894; Winstone 1981 (61)).

Fig 53. Pear Tree Cottage, Park Lane, 1950s

No house is shown here on the c.1710 revision of Millerd's map; from the ratebooks it appears to have been built c.1728.

Occupancy from the ratebooks:

1728 Edward Holder house and garden void, 1730 Thomas Harris house and garden in the Park, 1746 John Barnstable for house and garden, 1756 George Baskerville, 1770 Thomas Tesdale.

At the corner with Upper Church Lane, no. 32 Park in 1775 (demolished)

Reciting an earlier survey or deed a description of the Earle family estate in 1761 refers to a tenement with garden adjoining, near the Park, of Moses Deane or his tenants (University Deeds 251). Entries in the ratebooks confirm that this was later no. 32 the Park (see below). No illustrations of this property prior to its rebuilding c.1780 have been traced.

By 1784 this was the part of the premises of Richard Hill held by John Edwards blockmaker (abuttals from nos. 1–4), one of three new houses built c.1781–4 by Hill (PStM/Land Tax). For the earlier history of this property see also under nos. 8–12 Lower Park Hill.

Occupancy from the ratebooks:

1698 Joshua Woolnough for Mr Dean's house, 1703 Moses Dean for Hodge's garden, 1705 Joseph Bundy for Moses Dean's house, 1706 Capt. Hardy, 1708 Capt. Richard Burgess, 1734 Scrill void, 1735 Richard Burgess snr., 1740 Mrs Burgess, 1758 void, 1760 Thomas Bidwell, 1764 James Jefferies, 1766 Hannah Camplin (at no. 32 in 1775; held a tenement, garden, stable and premises in 1780), 1781 Richard Hill's 3 new houses unfinished, 1784 occupied by John Francis, John Edwards and George MacDonald.

Stile Lane

No. 1 (demolished)

Structures are shown on this plot on the 1828 map, but no illustrations of these have been traced. In 1664 this was the part of the Hill Ground enclosed with a wall leased by Isaac Harper gent. to Thomas Price shipwright, taken out of a ground then late of William Ballard bookseller; Ballard held the property on the south side of Medical Avenue (see Medical Avenue, above). The sequence of entries in the hearth tax and later returns indicates that by 1668 the property was held by Giles Case (see below). By 1690, when Ballard's ground was now of Henry Jones clerk, Price had built a tenement on the ground, the property now leased by Isaac Harper gent. to John Bound of Pill, shipwright, the lease renewed in 1701 (8016(22,29); the rent was 25s p.a.). In 1784 this was described as the garden ground of Samuel Whitchurch (abuttals from nos. 2–3).

Occupancy from the ratebooks:

1668 Giles Case 4 hearths, 1679 Giles Case, house and garden, 1689 Giles Keys (from position in assessment), 1695 John Bound, void, 1698 Samuel Tilley, 1713 Samuel Shawe, 1718 Lady Dodellstone, 1723 Capt. Symes, 1725 Mr Lewis, 1727 Capt. Foord, 1732 Mr Tustin, 1734 Mrs Hodges widow, 1764 Revd. Joseph Browne, 1766 – Combe, 1770 Sarah Ford.

Nos. 2 and 3 (demolished)

A house on the west side of the plot is shown on the air photograph of March 1935 (Aerofilms 40790). This was evidently of three bays with three hipped roofs set behind a parapet to the garden side, gabled on the west or boundary side. This was probably the 'summer house' built there in the early eighteenth century, originally with three gables to the garden side, modernised with a parapet and hips to the roofs at a later date, in exactly the way that the 'Manor House' in Royal Fort was modernised (see above).

Together with no. 4 this was the ground called the Little Park, formerly extending from the boundary of Thomas Price's property (see no. 1 Stile Lane) up to the boundary of Little Park, since enclosed, together with the dwelling house and buildings erected there, the last of William Donning or his tenants (University Deeds 251, a description of the situation in the later seventeenth century in an abstract of title for 1751).

This was part of the Little Park leased to James Donning in 1701; by 1731 Donning had 'divided the said ground' and had made two gardens. In 1731 one of these, on which he had built a summer house, was leased to John Pursell soapboiler by Robert Earle, executor of the inheritor of Harper's estate (8016(36)). In 1733 the last two entries for rates paid in 'the Park' were for Mr Purcel's garden and for Mrs Jones (St Michael's Scavenging Rates, 1733).

In 1746 this was the plot of ground 'with a small tenement or summer house thereon erected', leased by Harry Earle to Purcell. From 1776 it was leased by William Benson Earle to Isaac Mills chaser. This lease was renewed in 1784, the accompanying plan showing the occupancies or ownerships of the adjacent plots; on the east was Back Lane, later Stile Lane, on the west and south the garden and premises late of – Birkin and now of Samuel Whitchurch, on the north the premises late of – Rogers widow and now of George Williams gent. (A22026/1).

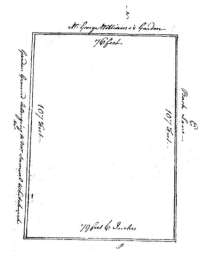

Fig 54. Nos. 2-3 Stile Lane, 1784

Occupancy from the ratebooks:
1679 Mr William Dunning, house void (with reference to both nos. 2–3 and 4 Stile Lane), 1689 Mr Dunning's garden (now just nos. 2/3), 1698 John Donning, 1706 James Dunning esq., 1723 John Purcell's summer house and garden, 1758 John Lowles' summer house and garden, 1764 Benjamin Watkins, 1771 William Thomas, 1772 Isaac Mills.

No. 4 (demolished)

At the northeast corner of the garden as shown on plan of 1808 was a 'house conveyed and belonging to John Parsons' (University Deeds 243). The house is shown on a drawing of the 1890s or early twentieth century by Loxton (BCL Loxton drawings 1761 X), on a photograph of 1932 (Winstone 1979 (107)) and on an air photograph of March 1935 (Aerofilms 40790). A steeply pitched roof and gables to the chimney stacks on the Stile Lane side indicate that it was probably of the seventeenth century or earlier; this was probably the

Fig 55. No. 4 Stile Lane, by Loxton

dwelling house of William Donning or his tenants mentioned in a lease of the seventeenth century (University deeds 252, reciting earlier leases, see Little Park above).

To the west were two houses built c. 1807; these are shown on the air photograph of March 1935 (Aerofilms 40790). In the southwest corner of the garden was a fourth property, shown as a house of one room in depth on the plan of 1808, extended northwards by 1828.

In 1786 the first of the above was the dwelling house, wash house and two gardens formerly of Mary Jones widow, after of John Ross, since of Richard Rogers gent. and now of Ann Williams wife of George Williams, conveyed in 1786 by William Benson Earle esq. to Mr Richard Hill. Then lately occupied by William Farr and Richard Hill, this contained in length on the north-west against Tyndalls Park 86ft, on the south-east against the tenement occupied by Isaac Mills tinplate worker 79ft (i.e. the preceding entry), on the north-east against the road or lane 104ft 6ins, on the south-west against the garden ground of Samuel Whitchurch 110ft (University deeds 243, bundle 1, the measurements given in the deed enabling the location to be precisely identified). In 1807 Richard Hill sold the property, now occupied by Mary Grumly widow, to George Watts, plumber; Watts subdivided the property as

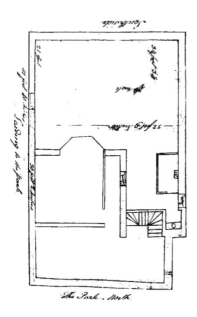

four separate units, building the two
new houses in the north-west corner;
these are show on a plan in the deed
of 1808 for the sale of southernmost
part. Access to the new houses was
through an enclosed way and then
through the gardens; the plan shows
also the stile or gate into Tyndall's
Park.

Occupancy from the ratebooks:

1679 Mr William Dunning, house
void, 1689 Mr Hassell's house
(from position in assessment), 1695
Samuel Wallis mayor, assessed for
9 windows, 1716 Capt. Christopher
Jones, 1723 Capt. Weston, 1727 Mrs
Mary Jones (at 'Park Gate' in 1736),
1748 Capt. Weston, 1750 Capt. Ross,
1758 Mrs Gwyer, 1764 Richard
Rogers, 1770 Mrs Ann Rogers.

Fig 56. No. 4 Stile Lane, plan of
1808

Upper Church Lane, north side

House numbers are shown on a plan of 1878 (University Deeds 251); for
properties on the south side of Upper Church Lane see Lower Church
Lane, north side.

**Nos. 1–4 (together with the frontage to Lower Park Hill), no. 1 Back
Church Lane in 1775 (demolished)**
Tracing the history of this property through the ratebooks and assessments
has shown that the house which stood here was substantial, assessed for
nine hearths by 1668 and for 16 windows in 1695. Reciting a much earlier
description, the property was described in 1761 as the tenement and
gardens formerly of Jonathan Blackewell and then late of William Atwood
merchant (University Deeds 251). A small part of the site was recorded
archaeologically in 1997 (Erskine 1997a and b).

By 1660 this was the property of Jonathan Blackwell, a wall built by him
adjoining the property of Edward Tyley (see nos. 8–14 Lower Park Hill). In
1668 and 1673 this was probably the house of Capt. or Jonathan Blackwell
assessed for nine hearths, by 1679 the house and garden of Mrs Blackwell
(F/Tax/A/1 and 4). Jonathan Blackwell evidently also owned the garden on
the lower and opposite side of Upper Church Lane; this would have

preserved the open view from his house, and explains why no house comparable to Rupert House or Llan House was built on that plot (see nos. 1–3 Lower Church Lane). By 1689 Blackwell's house was held by William Atwood, assessed for 16 windows in 1695 (F/Tax/A/5/StMi(a)).

In 1754 this was the property leased by Harry Earle to William Seede apothecary, a capital messuage or tenement, outhouses, buildings, gardens, coach houses, stables and premises adjoining, then in the possession of Mary Thomas widow, bounded on the east with a tenement then in the possession of Mary Burges spinster and on the west with a messuage and small tenement then of John Cheston baker and a coach house garden and stables over the way opposite then of John Brickdale esq. The house was rebuilt c.1758 (see ratebooks below).

In 1780 this was the property late of William Seede; a part 15ft wide at the south-east corner was the tenement now of Martha Jones spinster, the greater part of the frontage to Upper Church Lane being the house and garden formerly of Seed and now of Martha Jones spinster (abuttals from nos. 12–14 Lower Park Hill, shown in plan). In 1784 this was the tenement with garden ground, back kitchen and other buildings late of William Seed and now of Mary Seed widow, together with an adjoining tenement late of – Crawford and now of – Hale mariner, held by William Seed from the Earle estate by leases of 1754 and 1768, now conveyed by William Benson Earle to Mary Seed; to the north in 1784 were the gardens and premises of Richard Hill now held by William Pritchard yeoman and George MacDonald mariner, to the east Hill's premises fronting Upper Church Lane held by John Edwards blockmaker (A22026/1, annotated 'Q Coulson', with plan endorsed).

Occupancy from the ratebooks:

1668 Capt. Blackwell assessed for 9 hearths, 1679 Mrs Blackwell for house and garden, 1689 Mrs Blackwell, 1695 William Atwood assessed for 16

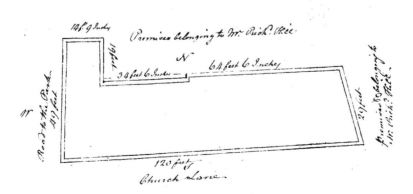

Fig 57. Nos. 1–4 Upper Church Lane, 1784

windows, 1696 household listed, 1723 Susanna Atwood, 1731a Mr Iliff, 1739b Thomas Grapper, 1742 John Thomas (in 1748 and tenants), 1755 William Seed's new house, 1756 Nathaniel Wraxall, 1764 Miss Cobb, 1766 – Orm, 1768 William Seed for his house, at no. 1 Back Church Lane in 1775.

For no. 5, at the corner with Park Lane, see Park Lane above.

Vine Row

Vine Row was developed as a row of fifteen houses from 1715 onwards; no. 18 was possibly later divided or rebuilt as two houses. The first building leases were granted to George Tully, house carpenter, for no. 9/10 and 13–16 in December 1715, those for 13–16 being regranted in August 1717. On these plots Tully was to build 'good, handsome and sufficient houses and pitch or cause to be pitched the said new intended street'. Nos. 9/10 to no. 17 were completed by c.1725; no. 18, possibly a subdivision of no. 17, was occupied from 1732.

The houses to the north-east of no. 9/10 were known as 'Earle's eight tenements', owned and leased by the Earle estate; no. 7 was occupied from 1730 onwards. The remaining houses had been commenced by 1732 but were mostly not occupied until 1739 or 1740. All are now demolished.

Nos. 1–8

These houses are shown in the distance on a photograph of 1952 (Winstone 1950-1953 (117)).

No. 9/10

No. 9/10 is the best recorded house in Vine Row. As the widest house and with a lantern to the roof it was more photographed and drawn. It was also the first house in the row to be completed, 'new erected' in 1717 when an additional plot within Tinkers' Close was granted to Tully by Robert Holmes. The completed house and garden behind were conveyed by Tully to Capt. Christopher Jones in 1720, the house itself now occupied by Thomas Phelps shipwright.

Nos. 11–18

These houses are shown in the distance on a photograph of 1952 (Winstone 1950-1953 (117)).

Occupancy from the ratebooks:

No. 1

1732–8, five and then seven houses void, 1739 Charles Mayes, 1742 George Goodman, 1744 William Hopkins, 1752 Richard Baily, 1762 Thomas Garston, 1768 Watkins, 1770 John Rawlins

No. 2

1732–8, five and then seven houses void, 1740 void, 1742 Mr Horsly, 1746 Mrs Horsly, 1748 Mrs Russell, 1750 Elizabeth Green, 1762 Thomas Place, 1764 Joshua Williams, 1768 Richard Hazard, 1774 Sarah Nicholson, 1776 William Watkins

No. 3

1732–8, five and then seven houses void, 1739 Charles Lake, 1742 John Frape, 1746 – Kersey, 1748 John Rowland, 1754 Edward Jenkins, 1766 Mark Noble, 1770 Abraham Hooper, 1772 William Davis

No. 4

1732–8, five and then seven houses void, 1738 void, 1746 Henry Williams, 1766 – Paine, 1770 Mr Somerton, 1774 Edmund Reece, 1776 James Webb

No. 5, no. 25 Park in 1775

1732–8, five and then seven houses void, 1740 John Cadwell, 1742 Ann Prosser, 1754 John Cook, 1766 Esther Cook, 1772 Ann Noble

No. 6

1732–8, five and then seven houses void, 1740 void, 1742 John Lewis, 1746 – Griffiths, 1748 Thomas Grapper, 1750 Capt. Foy, 1752 Richard Griffiths, 1754 Sarah Ford, 1770 James Edwards, 1774 widow Edwards

No. 7

1730 William Thomas, 1760 Mary Thomas

No. 8

1722–8, five and then seven houses void, 1739 Capt. Arnold then Dr. Jeremiah Swaile, 1746 Walter Perry, 1748 Stephen Yem, 1750 William Edwards, 1752 William Welch, 1758 – Prosser, 1760 – Carpasteen, 1762 Robert Simpson, 1766 Mrs Old, 1768 – Tovey, 1772 Henderson then Charles Webb

No. 9/10, no. 21 Park in 1775

1723 exec's of Jones, new house void, 1725 Mr Hobhouse void, 1727 Mr JohnTyler, 1742 Thomas Jones esq.

No. 11

1723 new house void, 1725 Ralph Kenvill, 1727 widow Skinner, 1728 Capt. Howell, 1732 Grace Bridget, 1736 Hugh Lawrence, 1740 James Lewis, 1742 Mrs Balme, 1764 Mrs Farnell, 1774 James Chilcott.

No. 12, no. 19 Park in 1775
1723 Mr Coates, 1725 Capt. Mullington, 1734 Mr Stokes, 1736 Capt. Arnold, 1738 Capt. Titus, 1740 void, 1742 Mrs Packer, 1758 Joseph Davis, 1760 John Davies, 1764 Samuel Ellis, 1772 Mr Henderson, 1774 Mrs Couzens, 1776 Samuel Willcocks.

No. 13
1723 void, 1725 Charles Harford, 1727 Richard Brown, 1730 Capt. Owen Arnold, 1736 Capt. Ross, 1738 Mr Slyton, 1740 Capt. Titus or Tilehirst, 1748 Peter Jones, 1750 widow Jones, 1754 Mrs Titus, 1764 Mrs Tishurst, 1770 Robert Combs, 1774 Peter Wade.

No. 14, no. 17 Park in 1775
1723 Capt. Forrest, 1725 William Hart, 1727 void, 1730 Vincent Walter, 1735 Capt. Ross, 1736 Mr Cottle, 1740 John Slayton, 1744 – Hannington, 1746 Nathaniel Thomas, 1750 Richard Horsley, 1754 Mrs Rebecca Lewis, 1756 Charles Baker, 1760 Thomas Jones [owner], 1762 William Purnell, 1764 William Barkley, 1768 David Barclay, 1772 Mary Hall.

No. 15, no. 16 Park in 1775
1723 Tully's house void, 1725 Jones tidewaiter, 1727 Henry Simpson, 1746 Elizabeth Simpson, 1760 Robert Simpson, 1772 Robert Bennett, 1774 John Hurne.

No. 16, no. 15 Park in 1775
1723 Tully's house void, 1725 Mr Simpson, 1727 Peter Jones, 1732 Edward Kendrick, 1774 Mary Kendrick.

No. 17, no. 14 Park in 1775
1723 void, 1725 Capt. Forrest or Hobhouse, void, 1727 William Gadd, 1728 Robert Gadd, 1730 Edward Kendrick, 1732 Peter Jones, 1750 William Green, 1752 William Edwards, 1758 void, 1760 Phillip Morgan, 1766 Jane Parrott, 1774 Richard Edwards.

No. 18, no. 41 Park in 1775
1732 John Green, 1740 widow Green, 1750 Mary Dollarhide, 1766 Betty Roberts, 1770 John Berry, 1772 William Sampson, 1774 Betty Roberts, 1776 Thomas Dickinson.

9. PARK ROW

One of the earliest references to the road which is now Park Row is that in a deed of 1566, referring to 'the way leading from the town towards Clifton' (00351(2)). By that date several houses had already been built in the separate land parcels uphill of Park Row, most identifiable as the houses of wealthy citizens. These are described here from west to east along the north and uphill side of Park Row (Figs.9–12).

The numbering of the houses in Park Row is first given in Sketchley's directory of 1775. Correlation of the directory with the rates for the parishes of St Augustine and St Michael shows that Park Row west of its former intersection with Griffin Lane was then known as Red Lodge Street (incorrectly correlated with Lodge Street in W.J.Jackson's rearrangement of Sketchley's directory). The street numbering recorded in nineteenth-century deeds for Park Row appears to use Sketchley's numbering. Here the present day numbers are utilised where shown on the Ordnance Survey plan; former street numbers and descriptive names are also used or noted where appropriate.

West of no. 29 (demolished)
This property was formally separated from Cantock's Close in 1802, now occupied by four coach houses and rooms over the same (05565, including plan; more detailed plan of coach houses is in 05566). The property was purchased for the widening of Park Row in c.1868, and remained open ground in 1884 (Ordnance Survey 1884).

Now no. 29, in 1775 no. 7 Red Lodge Street (demolished)
No illustrations of the buildings occupying this plot before the street widening of c.1868 have been traced; plans indicate the presence of a large two room deep house with a bay window at the rear, demolished for the road widening of c.1868 (05566).

In 1463–4 this was the house and garden of the Corporation on St Michael's Hill leased to John Barret for a yearly rent of 4s (GRB 4, 27). In

Fig 58. Park Row, 1864: from left to right above Park Row are nos. 8 and 9 (semi-detached pair), no. 12 (gabled), and nos. 13 and 14 (both eighteenth century), then no. 15 Lunsford House, and finally no. 16

1566 this was the garden and barn on St Michael's Hill next to the way leading from the town towards Clifton between a garden sometime of John Sherpe and now of the proctors of St Mary Redcliff on the east and 'a style beinge a certaine lane leadinge to a close of the Abbot of St Augustyne of Bristoll called Cantock's Close' on the west part, 68 feet wide on the south, 210 feet in length, which garden and barn were then in the tenure of John Barret hallier and Joan his wife, granted by the Corporation to John Goodryche clerk; the measurements agree precisely with those of the curtilage of no. 29, prior to the widening of Park Row. In 1591 this was granted in fee farm at a rent of 4s by the Corporation to Chistopher Carye merchant, the garden and barn now in the occupation of William Stanlacke merchant (University Deeds 190, the rent still charged to no. 29 until 1837; 00351(2)). Mrs Lettice Cary held the property in 1627 (BRS 24, 90). By 1700 the property was held by Sir William Merrick, now described as an orchard and stable formerly of Christopher Cary (04238 fol.28). Both Cary and Merrick owned the house or lodge to the east (see next entry).

By 1812 the property was late of James Hughes gent. It was then stated that the barn 'was many years ago pulled down and a capital messuage or dwelling house, coach house and stable with other buildings have since been erected'. From the evidence of the ratebooks this house was probably first occupied c.1709.

Occupancy from the ratebooks:

1709 James Warren, 1724 Mr Pyne, 1727 Capt. Wathen, 1734 Mrs Phippen, 1738 Mrs Pritchard, 1739 Richard Rogers, 1746 Capt. Jackson, 1752 Sarah Sheppard, 1756 Mr Pope, 1758 Charles Haythley, 1762 Nathaniel Foy, 1765b – Norman, 1768 Miss Nash, 1775 John Mills, at no. 7 in 1775.

Nos. 8–13 Park Row (as numbered in 1877), in 1775 nos. 8–11

Red Lodge Street (demolished)

No. 11 Park Row is shown on an air photo-graph of March 1935, by which date no. 10 had been replaced by modern factory buildings (Aero-films 47090). It was recorded again on a photograph of July 1957 (Winstone 1988 (254)). From the correlation of these two photographs with the plan of 1911 it

Fig 59. No. 10 Park Row, gabled house on left, 1957

can be suggested that the earliest part of the house was the upper and slightly wider part projecting into what had been Cantock's Close. This was a structure probably of one room on each floor, of two storeys and an attic, with a steep gabled roof, of the seventeenth century or earlier. The lower part of no. 11 was probably of two rooms in length, of two storeys and an attic, with gables to the attic windows, of the seventeenth century or earlier.

No. 10 was an extension of this house to the south. No information is available for the appearance of no. 10 (a small part of the house wall may survive).

The seventeenth-century or earlier house and the curtilage of nos. 8–11 Park Row can be identified as the property which in 1548 belonged to Mede's chantry in St Mary Redcliff, comprising a garden held by Thomas Moore, a garden and 'le Lodge' held by Maurice Cradogge and a close held by Nicholas Thorne (PRO E318/33/1845). In 1566 this was the garden sometime of John Sherpe (whose daughter Elizabeth married Richard Mede), now of the proctors of St Mary Redcliff (abuttals from house to west, GRB 3, 171). Being part of the endowment of Mede's chantry, the property must have existed as a separate entity by c.1491 (PRO PROB11/Milles/45).

By 1662 this was the house of Christopher Cary, in 1673 the property granted by Margaret Carey widow to Edward Baugh linen draper, in 1688 granted by Sir William Merrick and others to Elizabeth Langton and others, passing to Samuel Cox in 1709, granted by Stephen Hodges and others to Thomas Gibbs by 1731.

Gibbs was responsible for subdividing the property. By 1749 there were six houses owned by Thomas Gibbs and bequeathed to his son Richard, by 1760 of Richard's daughter Mary, then now or late of Henry Bodmin, Ann Smith, Joshua Astley, the Revd. Mr Gautia, Madam Braine and James Bridges, by 1766 of Mr Prothero, Richard Page, Henry Bodmin, Capt. MacNeal, George Luther and Mrs Smith, by 1767 of Robert Bridle, Henry Bodmin, the Revd. John Davis, Julius Derecourt, William Dimock and the Revd. Gotier, the house and garden of Thomas Dymock merchant on the east, that of John Mills vintner on the west, Cantock's Close on the north (05569). The new houses built by Gibbs are described below.

On maps of 1736 and 1742 an entrance on the north side into Cantock's Close is shown as 'Mr Gibbs door' (DC/E/40/48/112 52139 and DC/E/40/48/2 52131); the property is shown as 'late Gibbs' on a plan of Tower View in 1796 (see below).

No. 10 was by 1796 the house and garden of Mrs Mary Williams (abuttals from no. 11). In 1877 it was the tenement with a large walled garden, hot house etc., formerly of Mary Williams, late of Robert Nation Gillard, the occupier in 1837, and late of William Heaven; by 1911 it had been renumbered as no. 15 (University Deeds 240).

No. 11 was by 1796 the tenement and garden on Stony Hill formerly of Margaret Carey widow, Thomas Gibbs and then of William Henwood

Excise Officer, bounded on the east by the garden of Thomas Blackwell (no. 14 Park Row) and on the west by the garden late of John Mills vintner (now no. 29 Park Row), on the north by Cantock's Close and on the south by the house and garden of Mrs Mary Williams. In 1877 no. 11 was described as the tenement and garden on Stoney Hill formerly of William Henwood officer of Excise, William Cowley paper maker and stationer, Samuel Turner, Captain Davis, Edward Nicholls cooper, Thomas Gillford (there 1837), then of his widow, bounded on the east by a garden formerly of Thomas Blackwell esq. since of Danvers Ward surgeon, after of Thomas Crossman, in the occupation of John Hall glazier and late of Mrs Harriet Heaven widow (no. 14 Park Row), on the west by a garden formerly of Ralph Montagu esq. and now of Joseph Kelson surgeon (the owner of the later no. 29 Park Row in 1851), on the north by Cantock's Close and on the south by the tenement formerly of Mary Williams since of Mr Gillard twine maker (no. 10 Park Row) and now or late of Henry Shepherd (University Deeds 240 with map showing house numbers).

Occupancy from the ratebooks:

1662, 1668 and 1673 Christopher Cary assessed for four hearths, 1679 Miss Baugh, 1689 Sir William Merrick, 1696 Sir William Merrick for house, garden and part of Cantock's Close, 1705 Lady Merrick for house and garden, 1706 Joseph Bundy, 1718 Mr Gibbs void, 1723 Mrs Cox void, 1724 Mrs Long and Mr Masters 1728 Mrs Long and Rose Millett, then:

No. 10 ?

1730 Mr Nelmes, 1734 Capt. Dolman, 1734 Madam Long, 1735 Jones, 1737 Philip Watkins, 1740 James Russell, 1744 Thomas Gibbs, 1748 Mrs Farrell, 1749 Josiah Ashley, 1762 George Luther, 1766 Revd. Mr Gothier, 1772 Capt. Emms, 1776 David Jones, 17789 Charles Bullock, 1783 John Hartnell.

No. 11 ?

1740 Honor Long, 1756 William Turner, 1760 Mrs Smith, 1764 William Fitzherbert, 1766 Mr Dymock junr., 1768 Richard Lowe, 1772 Jacob Moore, 1783 Mrs Moore.

Nos. 8 and 9 Park Row (as numbered 1877), in 1775 nos. 8 and 9 Red Lodge Street (demolished)

These two houses are shown on the 1828 map with gardens extending southwards to Park Row. They were built c.1729 when Thomas Gibbs mercer leased from the city the ground 'before two houses on Stony Hill', were first occupied c.1730, and are shown most clearly on a photograph of 1864 (09082(1) fol.408; Winstone 1972 (9)). Each was of three storeys and of two rooms in depth, one of the earliest pairs of semi-detached houses known of in the city.

There was no house occupied here before c.1729 (see below, ratebooks). In 1794 the westerly of the two houses had formed part of the estate of Margaret Twine, was subsequently occupied by Sarah Seyer and was then sold by the Revd. Samuel Seyer to Mr John Howell in 1812. Elizabeth Thompson widow was described as the late occupant of the easterly house. By 1837 both houses were owned by John Howell. By 1855 the westerly was no. 8, the easterly shown as no. 9 on a conveyance of 1870 when it was purchased by William Heaven (University Deeds 240; 1837 survey). Heaven's purchase was from the Bristol Local Board of Health, which had purchased both properties to facilitate the widening of Park Row. The two houses were not demolished until the 1950s or 60s.

Occupancy from the ratebooks:

No. 8
1730 – Marshall, 1732 Madam Long, 1735 Capt. Thomas Dolman, 1748a Thomas Gibbs, 1748b Capt. West, 1749b Revd. Mr Tucker and then Revd. Mr Sawyer, 1752 void, 1754 Mrs Findlay, 1756 Capt. Miller, 1758 Mr Bridges, 1761b Capt. Hector MacNeal, 1765b Revd. Mr John Davies (at no. 8 in 1775), 1783 William Seyer (the property now owned by Thomas Kington).

No. 9
1730 Honor Long, 1732 James Phelps, 1742 Henry Bodman, 1766 Mary Bodman, 1768 Mr White, 1770 Mr Benjamin Durston (at no. 9 in 1775), 1783 Elizabeth Thompson.

No. 12 Park Row (as in 1877), no. 10 Red Lodge Street in 1775, by 1911 no. 13 Park Row, Ethelbert House (demolished)
A tall gabled house, of three storeys and of a distinctly mid nineteenth-century appearance, is shown on a photograph of 1864; the location of the house is shown most clearly on Ashmead's map of 1828 (Winstone 1972 (9)). It was demolished for the widening of Park Row c.1868 (05569).

There was no house occupied here before c.1733 (see below, ratebooks). In 1796 this was the small tenement and garden formerly of Margaret Carey, after of Thomas Gibbs and then of Joseph Bowyer accountant, bounded on the east by a house of Mrs Louisa Bale, on the west by a passage leading up to Henwood's house (nos. 10-11). Behind it was a small garden with a summer house, then occupied by Thomas Fisher gent. (University Deeds 240).

Occupancy from the ratebooks:

1727 William Bond, 1728 Thomas Gibbs's garden, 1733 Mr Stocker, 1736 John Higley, 1742 Thomas Gibbs, 1744 Mrs Webb, 1746 Mrs Lewis, 1748

Thomas Gibbs, 1749 Sarah Sheppard, 1752 Mrs Kennedy, 1756 late Mr Counsel, 1758 Mrs Batchelor, 1760 Peter Gauter, 1762 John Savage, 1766 Mr Derracour, 1772 Thomas Vaughan, 1774 Richard Thomas, 1775 William May, at no. 10 Red Lodge Street in 1775).

No. 13 Park Row (as in 1877), no. 11 Red Lodge Street in 1775, by 1911 no. 11 Park Row, Bertha House (demolished)

There was no house occupied here before c.1725 (see below, ratebooks). A detached house of the eighteenth century, of three storeys and an attic, of two rooms in depth and c.30 ft wide, is shown on a photograph of 1864; the location of the house is shown most clearly on Ashmead's map of 1828 (Winstone 1972 (9)). It was demolished for the widening of Park Row c.1868 (05569).

In 1796 this was the house of Mrs Louisa Bale (abuttals from no. 12). In 1877 this was the property bounded on the east by land of Michael Crowe and agreed by him to be sold to William Heaven and on the west by land late of Samuel Bryant, then of William Heaven and now used as an industrial school (University Deeds 240).

Occupancy from the ratebooks:

1725 John Norman, 1734 Capt. Bond, 1735 Thomas Gibbs, 1742 Mrs Braine, 1764 Capt. Prothero, 1768 Robert Bridill esq., 1775 Edward Daniel, at no. 11 Red Lodge Street in 1775, 1779 Revd. Mr Bale.

No. 14 Park Row (as numbered in 1877) (demolished)

A detached house of the early eighteenth century, of five bays with tall sash windows and string courses at the first and second floors, is shown on a photograph of 1864; it was of three storeys and an attic, and was of two rooms in depth (Winstone 1972 (9)). Shown on Ashmead's map of 1828, it was demolished for the widening of Park Row c.1868 (05569).

In 1663 this was the house of Peter Rosewell woollen draper, an additional strip of land in front of no. 15 to accommodate a way up to no. 14 being leased from that date from the Corporation (04335 fol.2). Rosewell's principal house was evidently on Bristol Bridge (F/Tax/A/1). By c.1700 the additional strip of land was leased to George Morgan, providing a way up to the house in his own possession (04238 fol.29). Joseph Percival lived here from c.1727 to 1762; as a merchant he traded in Jamaica, Ireland and Europe, bequeathing £70,000 (PRO PROB11/885/138). Josiah Ashley lived here next, followed from 1764 by Thomas Dymock gent. (P/StMi/Land Tax). In 1775 this was the tenement with gardens adjoining, formerly of Thomas Dymock, conveyed by his executors to Robert Bridle esq., in 1781 granted by Bridle to Thomas Blackwell. By 1812 it was of John Lewis esq., now conveyed by John Blackwell of Bridgend to Danvers Ward surgeon, the owner and occupier in 1837, bounded on the east by a tenement and garden formerly of James Ireland, then of Samuel Whitchurch, on the west by a tenement formerly of Robert Bridle, a tenement and garden formerly of – Moore and another tenement of – (05580, the measurements and plans in the abstract of title and associated documents confirm the location).

In 1796 this was the house joined to the garden noted as Mr Blackwell's (abuttals from Tower View). Formerly of Thomas Blackwell esq. this was in 1877 since of Duncan Wood surgeon (probably the D Wood named as the owner in 1837), after of Thomas Crossman, in the occupation of John Hall glazier and late of Mrs Harriet Heaven widow (abuttals from no. 11).

Occupancy from the ratebooks:

1668 Robert Yeamans, 1673 his widow, assessed for seven hearths (from position in assessment), 1679 Capt. George Morgan, 1718 Gilbert Cobb, 1723 Mary Dighton widow, 1724 void, 1725 Joseph Percival, 1764 Thomas Dymock, 1775 Robert Bridle, at no. 12 Red Lodge Street in 1775, 1782 Thomas Blackwell.

Tower View

Tower View is a summer house of the later eighteenth century, built in Brandon Hill stone, originally standing within the north-west corner of a large walled garden, with prospects over both the city and Tyndall's park. It is now designated as of grade II in the statutory lists of buildings of architectural and historic interest.

The original summer house has been extended eastwards, the open arched entrance to the garden now infilled, with the interior totally remodelled. The north

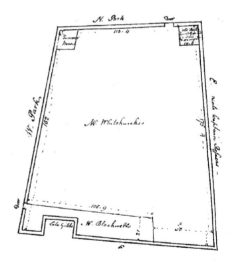

Fig 60. Tower View in 1796

wall of the eighteenth-century garden and a small part of the east wall remain. On the west face of the former summer house is the road sign for 'Woodland Rise'.

The enclosed garden of Tower View does not appear on Rocque's map of 1742 or on an estate plan of a year later ((DC/E/40/48/2 52131). In 1781 this was the half-acre plot, part of the six acres of Cantock's Close, now and for some time enclosed with a stone wall and used as part of the garden of James Ireland, and before that of Joseph Percival merchant (of no. 14 Park Row), now leased by Tyndall to James Ireland (of no. 15 Park Row) for 39 years, with a summer house and buildings thereon erected and with two doors into the close. In 1796 the garden was sold on a lease of 990 years to Samuel Whitchurch (of no. 15 Park Row). The plan endorsed on the deed is a critical document in understanding the context of Tower View and for identifying other properties in later eighteenth-century Park Row. On the east was the land late of Capt. Rosser. On the south the projecting part of no. 11 Red Lodge Street is shown as 'late Gibbs', the occupancy or ownership of no. 14 is revealed through an adjacent strip of the half acre plot being itself part of 'Mr Blackwell's', shown on the plans of 1883 and 1911 as part of that garden. The greater part of the garden held by Samuel Whitchurch can only have been linked to no. 15, Lunsford House.

In 1925 the half acre plot was sold by the Corporation to the University (University Deeds 243). The garden and summer house are shown on an air photograph of March 1935 (Aerofilms 47090). This shows also the wall within the larger plot, which in 1796 separated the gardens of Whitchurch and Blackwell.

Most of the archaeology of the garden has been removed in successive building works of the 1970s and 1990s. A small part must remain below and uphill of the road that now runs beneath Tower View.

No. 15, Lunsford House
Detailed architectural survey has shown that Lunsford House is of three principal phases. The projecting wing on the uphill side is of the nineteenth century. The central part is of the seventeenth century, totally rebuilt internally in c.1738–39. The part closest to Park Row is of c. 1738–39.

The early deeds for Lunsford House or its neighbours have not yet been identified; from the ratebooks its history can be untangled with difficulty. Before c.1738, possibly from c.1708, it seems to have been the house known as Caduggan's tenements. Since the house could be approached either from Medical Avenue or from Park Row, its position in the ratebook lists varies. It is possible that the route known as Medical Avenue in the nineteenth century continued further to the west, providing access originally to nos. 10/11 Park Row, the Merricks' house and earlier lodge. Before the construction of Thomas Gibb's houses in Park Row it is more easily identified, as the house beyond those of Sir William Merrick and Capt. George Morgan and their predecessors.

The reconstruction of c.1738–39 must have been undertaken for James Furney, who lived there only briefly, dying in 1741 (PRO PROB 6/117 (admon.)). The house and garden were of sufficient note to merit Rocque's attention; the house is shown on his map of 1742 in detail, though incorrectly, together with its garden, and as of J.P.Fruhr; his name is briefly recorded in the ratebooks. J.P. Fuhr or Fewer died in 1744 (PRO PROB 6/119).

Fig 61. Tower View in 2000 — note the blocked window
above the present window

Fig 62. Lunsford House in 2000

In 1828 Lunsford House was shown on Ashmead's map as being the Park Academy. By 1862 it was formerly in the occupation of James Tratman, then of his widow, and then or late of Frederick Chapple and now used as the Certified Industrial School for Boys (abuttals from Medical School). In 1925 this was sold by the Corporation to the University (University Deeds 243).

Behind Lunsford House but within its curtilage was the Medical School. Nothing is known of the history of the buildings on this part of the site; it could have formed part of a complex of buildings here from at least the late seventeenth century. In 1834 it was the property conveyed by Mary Perry, Joseph Whitchurch and Charles Gresley to Edward Clark, by 1862 the buildings known for many years past as the Medical School in the Old Park, with a strip of land 5ft wide and 4ft 6ins wide (University Deeds 243, abstract of 1902 with plan). In 1925 this was sold by the Corporation to the University (University Deeds 243).

Occupancy from the ratebooks:

Argued to be the rear part of Lunsford House – no entries after 1738
1668, 1673 John Hellier assessed for three hearths, 1689 widow Hellier and Arthur Sawier, 1703 James Peters soapboiler for widow Hickes's house, 1707 James Hutchings, 1708 Cadugan for late Hutchings, 1710 Capt. Scott for Cadugan, 1712 John Bradway two tenements, 1715 John Bradway or Mr Bundy, 1716 John Bradway, 1718 Mr Johnson, 1723 Powell and Noble, 1731 Mrs Sarah Gooding or Goodwin, 1732 Sarah Gooding and Richard Edmunds, 1733 Sarah Goodwin two houses, 1738 Mrs Goodwin as was now Mr Percival.

No. 15 Park Row, argued to be the site of the front part of Lunsford House before c.1740
1689 alderman John Hickes's garden, 1706 widow Hickes's garden, 1707 Henry Combe's garden, 1718 void, 1724 Mr [James] Furney's garden, 1739 Mr Furney's house and garden [with rents doubled], 1741 James Furney now Fewar [sic], 1744 Phillip Fuar (J.P.Fuhr esq. is shown as the owner of this house on Rocque's map of 1742), 1746 Samuel Randall, 1750 void, 1751 Revd Dr Tucker, 1766 James Ireland esq., at no. 14 Red Lodge Street in 1775, 1776 William Berkin for house and dairy.

No. 16, later the site of the Synagogue (demolished)
A detached house of the later eighteenth century, of four bays, is shown in part on a watercolour of 1824 and also on the photograph of 1864; it was of three storeys and an attic, and was probably of at least two rooms in depth (BRSMG M.2571 Winstone 1972 (9)). It is shown in outline on Ashmead's map of 1828, and was demolished for the widening of Park Row c.1868 (05572).

In 1665 this was the site of a little lane leading from Stony Hill up to a garden called 'Collonell Birches' then of alderman Jackson (abuttals from Stratton's house and garden, see below).

The plot is shown as separate from Lunsford House in 1742. By 1786 it was of Ann Brain spinster, by 1807 of Matthew Wright

Fig 63. Nos. 16 and 17 Park Row, detail from watercolour of the Red Lodge and Lodge Street, 1824

merchant (abuttals from garden to N of Park Row Asylum). By 1853 it was used as an institution for the instruction of the deaf and dumb (abuttals from Park Row Asylum).

Occupancy from the ratebooks:

The two houses later no. 16 Park Row
1668 possibly John Saffin, three hearths, 1673 two hearths, 1689 Samuel Clarke, 1695 widow Clark void, 1698 Arthur Sawier, 1700 Richard Leversedge, 1706 Jonathan Allen sugar baker, 1723 Henry Allen, 1732 Henry Allen's two houses, 1734 Thomas Brayne's two houses, then:

No. 16 Park Row (part of), not numbered under Red Lodge Street in 1775, probably to the rear of no. 15
1736a Mrs Shuter, 1740 Thomas Braine, 1760 Mrs Braine, 1762 Mrs Smith, 1782 Elizabeth Brayne.

No. 16 Park Row (part of), no. 15 Red Lodge Street in 1775
1736a Thomas Brayne, 1740 Capt. Pranent, 1742 Capt. Whitford, 1750 Thomas Gibbard, 1754 Madam Rishton, 1756 Capt. Lewis, 1758 Mrs Hall, 1772 Revd. Mr Beale, at no. 15 Red Lodge Street in 1775, 1779 Mrs Brown.

No. 17 Park Row, formerly no. 16 Red Lodge Street and later the Park Row Asylum, demolished and now the car park of the Buildings Maintenance Department

In 1596 this was possibly the garden of John Barker merchant (8016(8)). Certainly situated to the east of nos. 1–3 Lower Park Hill, it would then have formed part of the Little Park estate. Barker's house in Small Street was occupied by Elizabeth Gonning in 1669 (Suff. R.O., North Papers). In 1662 this was probably the garden house in St Michael's on which John Gonning esq. was assessed for two hearths (F/Tax/A/1).

In 1669 the front part was the plot of void ground over against the Red Lodge, 110ft long and 25ft wide, leased to Elizabeth Gonning, having her garden wall on the north side and the highway on the south. By 1700 this was of Lady North but in the possession of Mr French (04238 fol.28). From 1716 the lease was held by George Allanson gent., his dwellinghouse and garden now on the north (04335(5) fol.77), a new lease granted in 1828 (University Deeds 243). Built on this part of the property were in 1779 two small messuages and stables belonging to the Revd. Mr Cobb, and abutting the garden to the north, all shown on Ashmead's map of 1828 (abuttals from nos. 1–2 Lower Park Hill). The easterly of the two tenements fronting Park Row is shown on a watercolour of the 1820s. It was gabled end on to the street with hood moulds to the windows on the ground and first floors,

Fig 64. No. 17 Park Row, one of the two
houses in front of the main house

probably of the seventeenth century or earlier (BRSMG M.2561). Further back from the street, in the north-west corner of the garden, a larger building is shown on the 1828 map; this is shown partly on the watercolour of 1824, together with part of no. 16 Park Row (BRSMG M.2571).

The central part of the plot, earlier of Elizabeth Gonning and then of George Allanson (see above), occupied later by the asylum, was by 1776 the garden ground occupied by Rowland Williams, sugar-baker (abuttals from nos. 1–2 Lower Park Hill), in 1794 the freehold tenement nearly opposite the Red Lodge, for-merly of the widow Higgins, after of George Warrin, then of Rowland Williams esq., then of Sarah Lucas, the premises having formerly been purchased by George Alanson from Elizabeth Stroud et al. By 1853 it was late of Thomas Corey esq., and now void (University Deeds 243).

Occupancy from the ratebooks:
1662, 1668, 1673 John Gonning assessed for two hearths, 1679 Sir Robert Gunning house and garden, 1692 Sir Dudley North house and stable, 1695 William French assessed for 9 windows, 1698 William French esq. for house, stable and gardens, in 1700 styled 'merchant', 1704 widow Higgins in French's house, 1705 widow Higgins for Lady North's house, gardens, stables, 1711 void, 1712 George Allanson (in 1718 for his house, three stables, three tenements and coach house), 1723 Mrs Allanson, 1725 Dr Bonithorn, 1762 Rowland Williams sugar baker, at no. 16 Red Lodge Street in 1775.

BIBLIOGRAPHY

Maps

Ashmead, George C. and Plumley, John, 1828. A map of the City of Bristol and its suburbs, copies in Bristol City Library, Bristol City Museum and Art Gallery, the Bristol Record Office and the British Library

Donne, Benjamin, 1826. *A plan of Bristol, Clifton, the Hotwells etc. from an actual survey by B. Donne*, copies in Bristol City Library, Bristol City Museum and Art Gallery and the British Library

Millerd, James, 1673. *An exact delineation of the famous citty of Bristoll and suburbs thereof*, London and Bristol: John Overton and Thomas Wall, copies in Bristol City Library, Bristol City Museum and Art Gallery and the British Library

Millerd, James, c.1710. *An exact delineation of the famous citty of Bristoll and suburbs thereof*, London and Bristol: John Overton and Thomas Wall, revised and reprinted, copies in Bristol City Library, Bristol City Museum and Art Gallery and the British Library

Ordnance Survey, 1884. *City and County of the City of Bristol*, Sheets LXXI.16.13, LXXI.16.14, LXXI.16.18, LXXI.16.19, LXXI.16.23, LXXI.16.24 [at 1:500]

Ordnance Survey 1885. *Gloucestershire*, Sheet LXXI.16. [1:2500]

Ordnance Survey 1903. *Gloucestershire*, Sheet LXXI.16. [1:2500]

Rocque, John, 1742. *A plan of the City of Bristol*, London: John Pine, copies in Bristol City Library, Bristol City Museum and Art Gallery, the Bristol Record Office and the British Library

Other

BaRAS 1994. *Archaeological Evaluation of Park Row and Woodland Road, Clifton, Bristol, BA/C071*, Bristol: Bristol and Region Archaeological Services

BaRAS 1998. *Archaeological Desktop Study of Upper/Lower Church*

123

Lane, Bristol, Report No. 457/1998, Bristol: Bristol and Region Archaeological Services

Bettey, Joseph, 1997. *The Royal Fort and Tyndall's Park: the development of a Bristol landscape*, Bristol: Bristol Branch of the Historical Association, the University, Bristol

Bickley, F.B., ed., 1900. *The Little Red Book of Bristol, volumes 1 and 2*, Bristol and London: Hemmons and Sotheran & Co.

Bristol Archaeology n.d. *St Michael's Primary School, Bristol*, Bristol: Bristol City Museum and Art Gallery

Costello, Kieran and Burley, Richard, 1997. *Charity on Camera in Edwardian Bristol*, Derby: Breedon Books

Dawson, D., 1981. Archaeology and the medieval churches of Bristol, *Bristol Archaeological Research Group Review*, **2**, 9–23

Erskine, Jonathan G.P., 1997a. *St Michael's on the Mount Without ... Additional Class room Archaeological Recording During Construction*, Bristol: Avon Archaeological Unit

Erskine, Jonathan G.P., 1997b. Archaeological recording at St Michael's on the Mount Without, Upper Church Lane, Bristol, 1997, *Bristol and Avon Archaeology*, **14**, 55–58

Firth, C. and Leslie, J.H., 1925. The Siege and Capture of Bristol by the Royalist Forces in 1643, *Journal for Army Historical Research*, **4**

Greenacre, Francis, 1982. *Marine artists of Bristol, Nicholas Pocock, Joseph Walter*, Bristol: Bristol City Museum and Art Gallery

Ison., W., 1952. *The Georgian Buildings of Bristol*, London: Faber and Faber

Latimer Annals. *Annals of Bristol*, John Latimer, Kingsmead Reprints, 3 volumes, 1970

Leech, R.H., 1997a. The topography of medieval and early modern Bristol, part 1: property holdings in the early walled town and Marsh suburb north of the Avon, *Bristol Record Society*, **48**

Leech, R.H., 1997b. The medieval defences of Bristol revisited, in ed. L. Keene, 19–30, *'Almost the Richest City', Bristol in the Middle Ages*, London: British Archaeological Association Conference Transactions, **19**, 18–30

Leech forthcoming, volume on the town house and tenement in medieval and early modern Bristol

Manchee, T.J., 1831. *The Bristol Charities*, 2 volumes, Bristol: by and for T.J.Manchee

Mowl, T., 1991. *To build the second city, architects and craftsmen of Georgian Bristol*, Bristol: Redcliffe Press

O'Neil, B.H.St.J., 1960. *Castles and Cannon. A study of early artillery fortifications in England*, Oxford: Clarendon Press [posthumously completed]

Parker, G., 1929. Tyndall's Park, Bristol, Fort Royal and Fort House

Therein, *Transactions of the Bristol and Gloucestershire Archaeological Society*, **51**, 123–142

Patterson, R.B., 1973. *Earldom of Gloucester Charters, The Charters and Scribes of the Earls and Countesses of Gloucester to A.D. 1217*, Oxford: Clarendon Press

Roy, Ian, 1972. The Royalist Ordnance Papers – Part 2, Oxfordshire Record Society, **49**

Russell, James, 1995. *The Civil War Defences of Bristol. Their Archaeology and Topography*, Bristol: Privately printed

Sampson, W.A., 1912. *A History of the Bristol Grammar School*, Bristol: Arrowsmith

Seyer, Rev. S., 1821 and 1823. *Memoirs, Historical and Topographical, of Bristol*, 2 volumes, Bristol

Sprigg, Joshua, 1648. *Anglia Redivia; England's recovery being the history of the motions, actions, and successes of the army under the immediate conduct of his excellency Sir Thomas Fairfax ...*, London, reprinted Oxford 1854: Oxford University Press

Stainred, Philip, 1669. *A Compendium of Fortifications*, London: E. Cotes

Walker, David, ed., 1998. The Cartulary of St Augustine's Abbey, Bristol, *Bristol and Gloucestershire Archaeological Society, Record Series*, **10**

Winstone., J., 1990. *Bristol as it was 1963–1975*, Bristol: Reece Winstone Archive and Publishing

Winstone., R., 1961. *Bristol in the 1940s,* Bristol: Reece Winstone

Winstone., R., 1964. *Bristol as it was 1950–1953,* Bristol: Reece Winstone

Winstone., R., 1971. *Bristol as it was 1874–1866,* Bristol: Reece Winstone

Winstone., R., 1972. *Bristol as it was 1866–1860,* Bristol: Reece Winstone

Winstone., R., 1979. *Bristol as it was 1928–1933,* Bristol: Reece Winstone

Winstone., R., 1981. *Bristol as it was 1960–1962,* Bristol: Reece Winstone

Winstone., R., 1988. *Bristol as it was 1940–1960,* Bristol: Reece Winstone

Woodward, F.W., 1987. *Citadel. A history of the Royal Citadel, Plymouth*, Devon: Devon Books

INDEX OF PERSONAL NAMES

INDEX OF INSTITUTIONAL LANDHOLDERS

SELECT INDEX OF PLACES IN BRISTOL

*(Principal entries in **Property and Tenement Histories** shown in bold)*

133